Rapport
and success:

Human Relations in Music Education

Sister Cecilia Schmitt OSF

Foreword by Charles Leonhard

*God Bless you
Bernard !
Sr. Cecilia Schmitt*

Dorrance & Company • *Philadelphia*

To
the countless
students
who,
over the years,
have taught me
the secret
of
RAPPORT

*This book is a project of
the National Consortium for Humanizing Education*

R elationships build success

A cceptance of self, then acceptance of students

P upil-oriented music approaches

P ositive thinking in self-esteem

O bjective evaluation—not overpraise or underpraise

R ole of teacher: facilitator and catalyst

T eaching *people,* not just teaching music

Contents

To the Reader

As a reader of the manuscript of this book, I would like to share with subsequent readers that my study of these chapters was a most rewarding experience. I was very impressed and very deeply moved by the quality of the book. It is a most human, personal document, and should greatly enhance the awareness of educators—regardless of their teaching areas—of the potentials of the learning-teaching situation. It is in the author's delineation of the dimensions of the teaching-learning context that, I believe, she has made her most meaningful contribution.

Certainly rapport, respect, genuineness, empathy, and understanding are necessary psychological conditions in order that growth and learning can be facilitated. To acknowledge these as necessary, and possibly even sufficient, is to make a very meaningful commitment to a humanistic approach to education. The very lucid discussion of these conditions, with accompanying illustrations, represents a fundamentally significant contribution to educational strategy. It is, unfortunately, a seldom implemented strategy in formal educational settings. The vividness of the case illustrations adds considerable depth to the discussion of the necessary conditions.

Also, the author's focus on the needs of both the student and the teacher as mutually involved participants in the learning situation is a very significant contribution. Certainly, needs for security, safety, and self-esteem are basic to all our needs, but in the learning situation the participant, whether a teacher or a student (or more correctly, being a learner, whether categorized as a teacher or a student), has the opportunity for the satisfaction of higher-level needs such as cognitive understanding and self-actualization. It is in the satisfaction of these higher-level needs that the learner becomes spontaneous, creative, committed, and fully aware of his potential for being. It is in the author's emphasis on the achievement of the satisfaction of these higher-level needs that she focuses her attention on the potential for growth in the learning situation. The quest for the satisfaction of these needs should be a basic tenet in every teacher's construction of the potential of the learning situation. We all need each other in order to maximize each other's potential for growth and learning. Development for each of us is a process facilitated by meaningful interaction with significant others in our lives, and certainly students and teachers are very significant to each other in this regard. The author's focus on this dimension of the teaching-learning context is a sorely needed emphasis in education.

In my own growth as an academic and professional psychologist, I, too, have been profoundly influenced by the theorizing and research of the individuals to whom the author acknowledges her indebtedness, among whom are Carl Rogers, Abraham Maslow, Robert Carkhuff, and C. H. Patterson. In addition to these innovative theorists, I have been influenced by others who have attempted to spell out the implication of a humanistic orientation for the helping professions.

Consequently, this book gave me a strong feeling of confirmation of what I have come to believe are the optimal conditions for the facilitation of growth in oneself and others. While I was reading this book, I had a very profound feeling of the authenticity of this approach to teaching. I highly recommend this book to educators of all kinds because I believe it is a significant contribution to educational strategy.

Gordon Henley, Ph.D.
St. John's University
Collegeville, Minnesota

Foreword

American education is committed philosophically to the role of preparing students to live in a democratic society. It is widely recognized, however, that authoritarianism has often marred the operation of American public schools. Authoritarian attitudes and procedures fail to respect the unique personality and emotional makeup of the individual and by definition are antidemocratic.

Regimentation and standardization have all too often characterized the American educational program in general and the music program in particular. The interpersonal behavior of conductors of school music performance groups has often been conditioned by association over a period of years with authoritarian figures who exemplify the model of the military leader or that of the professional conductor. As a result, music educators too often take the authoritarian view that students and players in their organizations are means to their own ends, rather than the only view defensible in a democratic educational enterprise, that students and players are ends in themselves. Regimentation and standardization based on authoritarian dogma are paradoxical and absolutely indefensible in a music program, in view of the tremendous potential of music education for releasing the imagination and engendering the individual creativity of students.

Happily in recent years the forces of humanism in education have begun to challenge the arid and simplistic viewpoint of the behaviorists. Music education functions best as humanistic education, and music educators all over the country join forces with the humanistic movement.

Convincing evidence exists that a healthy emotional climate is one of the necessary conditions for successful learning in the classroom. It follows that one of the basic tools of a successful music teacher is the ability to establish an emotional climate and relationships with students conducive to learning and achievement.

This aspect of music teacher competency is frequently neglected in music teacher preparation programs. Great emphasis is placed on the development of musical skills and teaching strategies, but the prospective teacher is too often expected to develop his or her ability to relate to other people and to establish a healthy emotional climate in the classroom on the basis of intuition. It is assumed that the ability of the teacher to establish rapport with students represents a reflection of his personality and cannot be developed in any systematic way.

In her book *Rapport and Success,* Sr. Cecilia Schmitt challenges that assumption by laying down a blueprint for humanistic music education. Drawing on research in psychology, personality development, education, and, especially, on the astute common sense analysis of her own successful experience in working with students as human beings, she not only establishes a philosophic platform for humanistic music education but also presents and illustrates with charming anecdotes procedures for establishing rapport, for developing productive relationships with students, and for achieving the ultimate purpose of education in a democratic state—the enhancement of the unique personality of each individual and the flowering of his creative potential.

I am confident that music educators all over the country will join me in welcoming this book as a significant contribution to the professional literature of music education.

Charles Leonhard
Professor of Music
University of Illinois
at Urbana-Champaign

Preface

Although music educators are dedicated to their goal of engendering the skills, understanding, and appreciation of music, they often fail. Many times the reason for their failure is a lack of rapport; they do not relate meaningfully and convincingly to their students.

To these music educators, striving for success in their teaching, and to college students preparing to become music educators, this book offers concepts and attitudes underlying stimulating interaction between teacher and students. These pages present the essential means and skills of rapport plus many anecdotes illustrating related experiences, both good and bad.

A basic tenet central to this book is that when a student is in a situation of good rapport, he usually succeeds at his music. That is, when he feels respected he usually better performs, composes, and appreciates the expressive communication system which music affords. If a teacher takes the time and makes the effort to know student needs and to meet them, if he truly supports his student, the young person will hear the basic urge within him to grow and become a competent person and musician.

Unfortunately, however, music students are often inhibited by negative feelings such as anxiety, fear, and inferiority; and their instructors, not knowing what can be done, sometimes fail miserably in their teaching. Such teachers need to know the language of acceptance and compassion, which helps to uncover bad emotions and invites cooperation from the students. They need insights into the concerns of students; they need words that radiate respect; and, above all, they must have an authenticity of person which conveys to the students nonverbally their deep and sincere concern for the personal as well as the musical growth of the student.

A second basic tenet is that a music educator's role in a student's learning process is that of *teacher-facilitator*. Because of the peculiar nature of music, because it is a discipline and a personal, expressive communication system, there must be a balance between didactic and experiential modes of teaching. At times an instructor must lecture, demonstrate, and set standards of performance; at other times he must stand back and allow the student to become involved with the elements of music—its concepts, principles, and emotional implications.

In other words, the student is invited to be versatile and eclectic in his choice of methods of learning. Once he imitates; another time he memorizes. Now he catches on intuitively; then he deduces a logical rule or principle from information given by his teacher. At one time he learns kinesthetically, at another cognitively, and at still another he learns because of social pressure.

Because of the complexity of the human being in his act of acquiring knowledge and skill, the teacher who wishes to make a significant difference in the lives of his students sensitively watches their processes of thinking, follows their steps, carefully guides and reinforces their procedures, and helps them evaluate their conclusions.

Learning, then, is intimate; it is personal. No one can produce learning in another. A teacher may force the memorization of data; however, this set of facts may not be personally meaningful to students. Learning is, rather, an experience-oriented phenomenon and demands a certain quality of personal involvement in which the whole person, in his feelings and cognitive faculties, becomes unified in an all-pervasive change in his behavior or his attitudes.

Yet, to say that learning is intimate is telling only half the truth. Learning is also a social phenomenon. One human being is necessary to spark another's interest in learning; a human being must also be there to share the discovery of a student after his time of intimacy with the learning is over. When Billy, for instance, experiences his first tones on the trumpet, he cannot contain himself. He blurts out excitedly, "Hey! I can play these notes! Listen!" As he blasts away, all but breaking the eardrums of his teacher and peers, then and only then is this part of his learning experience complete. The same is true of all learning. Adults can read books and intellectually lay hold of new truths and perspectives. It is usually only when they have expressed these insights to others, interacted socially with others, verbalized the ideas, and gained something of another's acceptance, that they feel fully comfortable with, and fully in possession of, such new cognitive gains.

Although the music educator who fulfills his role as teacher-facilitator stands back, to a certain extent, and allows his students to be self-directed, he does not permit them to become mediocre in their efforts or performance. Rather, the teacher who is warm, accepting, empathic, and genuine can instill into the students a responsible freedom, which stimulates them to develop their talents. For such students, learning is *their* goal, not the teacher's; expressive communication through music is *their* great aim, not that of the person they pay to guide them. Skills improve, and higher-level tasks such as creating and improvising take on new meaning when students take the initiative in their own learning.

The third basic principle is this: in order to educate well, a teacher must know the students with whom he is dealing. When he stops to look at them and to listen to them in order to find out where their expectations lie, he begins to understand that students are not usually attuned to their real needs. Rather, they are driven by superficial interests, wants, and desires and often expect their teachers to satisfy their whims.

Dedicated teachers who are skilled in the tools and techniques of rapport see the deep human needs for self-image, power, and security. They observe, for instance, that one student wants over-challenging material but what he really needs is an outlet for his sense of power. The young girl may want to be a soloist; but her real need is for the enhancement of her self-image, which she feels she can get through the applause of others. Students who want to play "with it" kinds of music are really concerned with acceptance by their peers.

Teachers who keep in touch with students' feelings, wants, and needs have their finger on the pulse of powerful motivating energy. Because they are keenly aware of the aims and goals of students on the one hand, and, on the other, are conscious of the possibility that music can be an effective means in fulfilling these students' needs, such teachers direct purposeful and meaningful educational programs successfully.

Educational programs designed to satisfy the whims of students will fail. To base music education on the flitting fancies of youth is folly. To pamper students by satisfying their superficial interests or flimsy fantasies is to take a road that leads nowhere. However, to ignore student concerns is also a serious mistake. The practice of ignoring student feelings drives young people out of music programs. Music educators have made both mistakes; they have gone to both extremes. There is a middle path—a music educator can lead his students to a rigorous and high-standard music program. But first the teacher must see with somewhat clear perception just who the students are and how their motivational systems of needs, wants, and feelings can be ignited and set to work.

This book does not propose answers to particular situations; it only tries to help the educator seek causes and find his own solutions. Since human behavior is dynamic, is never the same in any two people, and is never static, one task of the teacher is to find some way to perceive and respond to the dynamics in operation within both himself and his students. These pages give clues to the reader about the inner motivations, activities, and workings of human intellectual and emotional systems.

A further tenet is that the best students, the most creative and most highly original in interpretation, are those who are most at ease. When they are not fighting their teachers, not criticizing their peers, not dissatisfied with themselves, they are able to be inwardly open to their experiences in learning and expressing music. The educator who relates to his students, the person who possesses and practices the skills of rapport, can lead students to success.

During the last twenty-seven years, the author has worked with students of all ages in classrooms, in small groups, and in private study. This book is the fruit of her experience. It is also the product of personal research and the distillation of many ideas gleaned from books and articles on psychology, sociology, philosophy, and human relations.

It may seem quite unorthodox for a music educator to be writing on the psychology of human relations. It may seem unusual for a music writer to point to "inside-of-me" solutions to music education's problems. It may even be shocking to some to see a writer departing from the closed system of authoritarian teaching common to many music departments and studios. Yet, whether they have wanted to or not, known it or not, music teachers have always needed to be relational experts to some extent. Those who were able to enter into the minds and feelings of their students experienced the greatest success. Today's teachers, too, can succeed in leading students to aim realistically, work assiduously, and experience success when they take the pains to know the inner workings of a student and begin to relate to him. For this relating, teachers need "psychological small change" or specific skills for dealing effectively and humanely with minute-to-minute conflicts, angers, and disturbances.

The depth of approach to relating offered in this book is somewhat of a departure from the pragmatic approach in which a person, student or teacher, uses a thing or a person for what he can get from it. Commonly people say, "I take a bath," "I take a walk . . . a swim . . . a drink," "I take a music lesson." They use opportunities as a ritualistic person; they study in Europe to become famous; they get an advanced degree to get a better job.

On the contrary, this book speaks of relating to students for their own sake and not for the personal gains of the teacher. The educator who has good rapport does not use the flashy performance skills of students to prove his own worth. He does not aim solely at the lower-level skills such as good reading, rhythm and digital skills. Instead, the humanistic teacher relates so well to his students that he is able to aim at the higher-level skills of creative interpretation and artistic expression.

xv

The highest priority of the educator with a high regard for rapport is his estimation of the true value of the human person. In the teacher's respect for himself as an individual and in his warm acceptance of each student, just as he is, lies the message of prime importance in these pages. The teacher, knowing his own lovableness and his personal struggle to gain self-actualization, reaches out in love to the student in his need for an enhancement of self-worth and self-image as well as in his need to grow and mature as a musician. In doing this, the teacher, although he retains his role as teacher, treats the student as equally human. He sees in the student magnificent powers, highly individual characteristics, as well as unique beauty of person, which become a constant source of surprise and wonder to him.

Although respect for the individual student is a natural part of the behavior of a humanistic teacher, some may suspect that it is a shallow gimmick. Truly, rapport with students brings success to a teacher. Students are eager for an atmosphere where they feel stimulated and not pushed around, where they are evaluated realistically, neither too vaguely nor negatively. Naturally, students want to enter programs where they can exert their rights as persons and enjoy purposeful activity. Students join such programs, and they do not quit easily. They find that the teacher who accepts them brings out all that is best in them. They and their teachers not only enjoy a certain mutual trust and loyalty, but usually come to possess monetary comforts as well.

Because of these benefits, the humanistic music educator not only leads a self-fulfilling and rewarding life himself; he attains the goal of his profession more directly than the performance-oriented teacher. He can honestly say that by means of psychologically sound and respectful human relations he elicits the good will of students and that through guidance and discipline he develops their personal potential. The goal of music education is to lead the student to self-fulfillment in emotional maturity and in musical capabilities to perform, create, and enjoy music.

One of humanistic education's goals is to engender in the student a taste, a curiosity, and an aptitude for acquiring new learning.

Since humane relating fosters the free and full functioning of the learner, it prepares him for the leisure world of today's culture and equips him to cope as an educated person with the rapid transitions taking place currently in society.

The philosophy of this book places the focus of the music program on the fulfillment of the person. The author is hopeful that this rationale satisfies the goal of music education as given in the Declaration of the Tanglewood Symposium:

> . . . Education must now concern itself with the art of living, with building personal identity, and with creativity. . . .
>
> Music . . . reach[es] close to the . . . roots of man in his search for identity and self-realization.
>
> Educators must accept the responsibility for developing opportunities which meet man's individual needs. . . .*

Sr. Cecilia Schmitt
Little Falls, Minnesota
April, 1976

---

* "Tanglewood Symposium: Music in American Society," *Music Educators Journal* LIV (November 1967), p. 59.

Acknowledgments

I am deeply grateful to Dr. David Aspy for his time, effort, and caring concern. I want to thank Dr. Charles Leonhard and Dr. Gordon Henley for their contributions in the early pages of this book.

I wish to express my sincere gratitude to Dr. John O'Connor for suggesting the book and guiding me with gentle persistence. I also owe a debt of thanks to Dr. Leo Rolls, Dr. Edgar Turrentine, Dr. Boyd Purdom, Dr. Irvine Dubow, and Helen Bambenek for their ideas, criticisms, and suggestions.

My editor, Sr. Linnea Welter, OSB, and my proofreaders also deserve special credit. I want to thank Srs. Adeline and Venard for many hours of studying the manuscript. Also, I am deeply indebted to all my sisters, students, and friends who supported and encouraged me.

Rapport
and success:

Human Relations in Music Education

The Definition and Attainment of Rapport

WHAT IS RAPPORT?

> Rapport is a delicate balance of two persons
> dancing to one beat.

Mr. Rumpet came to his Monday teaching scene in an angry state. When Cindy, eighteen, walked into her lesson and announced indifferently that she had not practiced, he became highly annoyed.

"What do you mean, Cindy, you didn't practice?" he shouted. "What do you want to grow up to be, a bum?"

After more irate statements, he stopped. He paused and continued in a tone of genuine concern. "As you notice, Cindy, I am angry. But I am not just angry about you. Last night I became aware that I myself have really wasted my talents in one area. Today I am resolved to help you. I don't want you to make my mistake."

Cindy was perplexed. Her relationship with Mr. Rumpet had been superficial, and she was not deeply involved with her music. She had a habit of easily excusing herself from her practice. Now she was stunned by his honest admission of personal emotions as well as his determination to help her. She left and came back with a perfect performance and a changed attitude toward her teacher.

She knew then that she could relate to Mr. Rumpet. He was a human being.

Teacher-student rapport may begin with encounters like this one. By showing his true feelings and his genuine care and concern for Cindy, Mr. Rumpet could begin to bridge the gap between Cindy and himself.

Can Teachers Meet Students?

Good rapport demands that a teacher possess a keen sensitivity to students' feelings and needs as well as a deep concern for their rapid progress in attaining music skills. When Allen stops singing on page 3, for example, Mr. Smith senses that he is embarrassed about missing his notes, and drills his intervals. When Susie has not even tried to practice her flute assignment, Mr. Bohm does well not to simply label her as "lazy" but, instead, understands that she is afraid of her music and takes steps to raise her self-confidence. If fear and insecurity continue to eat away inside these students, they may soon drop out of the music program.

A deadlock in communication between teacher and student often comes when a teacher is determined to make a supposedly talented student "produce." The student is often not ready to meet what seems to him to be an unrealistic and overly rapid acceleration in his study of music. Frequently high school students wonder: "Am I being used to prove the excellence of my teacher? Am I a mere tool which my teacher uses to chisel out his own image? Is he interested in me or himself? This music is meaningless. Why should I continue?"

Through keen awareness of the feelings and needs of individual students, a sensitive teacher can avoid violation of a student's personhood. When a teacher is sensitive and respectful of students, he not only refrains from infringing on their rights, but he is alert to students' inner values, emotions, and goals. He can also channel the feelings of the students into their activities and intensify the dynamic and emotional level of performance.

2

In a situation where a teacher enjoys a one-to-one relationship with a student, the sensitivity can become extremely keen. For example, today I may want to teach ten-year-old Scott how to play minor scales. In the brief moment before I begin, I may become aware of these things: Scott comes in breathlessly, as if he had run all the way, his eyes flit around looking for adventure, and his eagerness for movement is quite evident. Having noticed this, I begin to present the scales as a movement, a "going to and a coming from" progression of tones. I an aware of who Scott is, what his receptivity allows him to learn, and how I can best engage his mental and emotional equipment.

The music educator who wishes to help his students grow focuses his attention on the well-being of individual students as well as on the common good of his class. To establish a climate conducive to growth, the teacher must show a genuine, warm acceptance of each particular student in the group. When he is sensitive to students' feelings and cares about their personal growth, the teacher becomes a catalyst who facilitates the merging of individuals into a cohesive unit bent on achieving a common goal. He stimulates the timid and challenges the self-confident. When a teacher is indifferent to his students as human beings, he misses his chance to help them grow as persons and possibly opens the door to discipline problems within the group.

> Rapport is like the fine needle which touches a
> record precisely at a point where the best music
> is waiting for release.

Although a teacher in good rapport with his students is sensitively aware and concerned about student needs, rapport itself has a broader meaning. Rapport is essentially the acceptance of the human dignity of the student and the willingness to help him grow in his own way. Good relationships begin when teachers acknowledge these facts. By unearthing the goals and values of students, a teacher can find the reasons for a student's behavior. Only after this can teacher and student develop a mutual understanding.

George, a clumsy high school sophomore, plays his cornet too fast and too loudly. During rehearsals he conforms enough to maintain his position as "first chair" because he can thereby wield power over the band. Although one natural reaction to George's behavior might be to "set him straight" by overwhelming him with authoritarian control, his teacher can maintain order and protect the rights and feelings of all the students without completely crushing George. This insightful teacher sees George as a power-hungry youth who has been given no sense of importance by society, school, or family. Although his thirst for power has been highly frustrated and he uses extreme methods to satisfy it, he is still a human being, striving to become what he feels he must, and deserving of respect.

Because this is true, the respectful teacher treats George as a human being, not as a machine which must produce what he, the teacher, expects. George is not merely a tool in the hands of his teacher. He is a unique person who experiences music in his own way. He is "good" not only when he conforms to traditional standards. He is most truly "good" when he expresses his own ideas and feelings through his music. A teacher with good rapport struggles with such a boy to help him fulfill his needs in ways that build, not destroy, group efforts. If, on the contrary, George were to feel labeled as a "bad" student, he would defy his teacher. The ensuing student-teacher relationship would, undoubtedly, be bad. But when the boy feels accepted as a worthy person whose conduct is erratic at times, he is willing to cooperate with group goals and change his behavior little by little.

While George is bragging about his facility on the cornet, Ann puts her oboe down and wonders just how she ranks as a person and as a musician. Because Ann is too poor to buy an instrument, she plays the school oboe. She is deeply grateful for the use of the instrument and practices well. But she is worried. Is she talented? Does she have a future in music? Does she really count as much as George?

Ann is not alone in suffering from an identity problem. All adolescents, to a greater or lesser degree, question their worth.

They wonder if they are just slaves of their parents, their teachers. Teenagers often rebel and are unsure of the motivations of their actions.

Another source of confusion for Ann is the dilemma caused by the contradictory evaluations her teachers make. One says, "Ann, you're an angel, wonderful! You'll become famous." Ann blushes and feels guilty when she is overpraised. How can she live up to all that? Another teacher complains, "Ann, don't you care enough to buy better reeds?" She feels that she is an unworthy person because she cannot afford things people expect of her.

Ann needs honest, realistic praise and evaluation of her work. She seeks specific remarks about her behavior, not about her personhood. "Direct praise of personality, like direct sunlight, is uncomfortable and blinding."[1] Ann adds up negative and positive remarks about her work; and, if these are fair and honest, she is free to estimate how worthy she is as a person and, sooner or later, discovers her true identity.

Allen, at sixteen, is a joy to the tenor section. That is, he is always on pitch and is quietly awaiting the downbeat of the director. But he is not a joy to himself. He is a compulsive perfectionist and nervously works to become a good performer because he fears that others will not accept him as a person. During class he finds no security in just being a relaxed and spontaneous young man.

A teacher primarily interested in the excellence of his choir would welcome Allen and praise him for his effort, and thereby reinforce his compulsive overachieving. On the contrary, the teacher who has good rapport with his student cares as much about the boy's personality as about his choir work. He praises Allen for his personal values and unique individual characteristics.

Another typical student is little Julie, sitting at her sixth-grade desk. Julie loves to dream. Her family and friends tease her about being a featherhead, and she delights in pretending that she is the heroine of the most recent book she has read. She finds it hard to concentrate and has a difficult time settling down to work. Her little head and her changeable heart seem impenetrable to the adult mind. What will she do next? What is she trying to "pull"? Her mischievous nature, supplemented by the tricks she has learned from books, renders her a most unpredictable child.

Julie realizes that she puts a strain on her teacher. She feels very sad at times because she does not understand her own behavior and her problem of alienating adults. She craves a teacher who can look past her outward conduct. She finds in the teacher who has rapport with her students an honest person who helps her see meaning in reality. With the encouragement of a loving and caring teacher, Julie may discover she is a highly creative musician and begin to enjoy working in the real world.

Jerry, eight, claps his hands and clicks his heels excitedly as his music teacher passes out the rhythm instruments. As she hands Jerry his castanets, a music teacher might say, "Now keep these quiet until I say you should play." Then, while Jerry and his classmates are wiggling with eager expectation of musicmaking, she might tediously present the logical system of counting which they neither understand nor appreciate.

The teacher in good rapport with his student, however, is alert to Jerry's need to use his energy and make sound. He understands that his mind is not capable of abstract thinking; so he keeps him involved in kinesthetic, movement activities. Because he accepts Jerry and his classmates just as they are and wants them to learn in their own way, he does not impose adult modes of thought upon them.

As George, Ann, Allen, Julie, and Jerry experience the sincere human acceptance and concern of their teacher, they respond with love and trust. To them this teacher is not merely a person who has the job of training them; he is a fellow human being who has the same kinds of human experiences they have. He knows them and has allowed his students to know him. Rapport breaks down the barriers and allows the students as well as the teacher to be natural, free, and creative in the educational process.

How can the teacher begin to develop rapport with students? Before he can relate to students helpfully, he must know how he feels inside. He must recognize that he is annoyed by Allen's nervousness and Julie's lack of attention. To cover up inner feelings by thinking, "I *should* like her," causes a phony relationship to develop and could cause the students to act worse than ever. Only by admitting to himself that he feels disgusted, threatened, or angered by students can the teacher begin to be honest in his relationship with them.

Secondly, he must want to relate. A teacher in good rapport with his students reaches out to them because he considers them worthy and lovable. Because he prizes them as autonomous human beings, he stimulates their capacity for self-direction, creativity, and growth as unique persons and as musicians.

> The warm, subjective human encounter of two
> persons is more effective in facilitating change
> than is the most precise set of techniques
> growing out of learning theory.[2]

THE QUALITIES OF GOOD RAPPORT

What, then, are the essential elements of successful teacher-student rapport? First, the teacher must approach the student in an honest and genuine way. He must know his own feelings and be authentic in conveying these to students. Secondly, he empathizes with his students; he attempts to experience their feelings and goals. Lastly, he reaches out in caring concern, supporting, accepting, and approving of his students.

A Nongenuine Teacher

Miss Perkins came into her general music class one March day and snapped a brisk "Good morning, class. Be quiet and listen. I am going to put up a chart analyzing a Beethoven symphony. I said *quiet!*"

Her students, however, were busy taking her emotional temperature. What was her problem? Why did her eyes have that angry flare? Why did she talk so fast, so loudly, and so vehemently? With all these disturbing unanswered questions, how could they listen calmly to Beethoven?

The class went from bad to worse. Miss Perkins's trembling fingers struggled with the chart, and soon she dropped it. The class laughed. Miss Perkins became furious. She drilled the symphonic themes by pounding them out forcefully at the piano and demanded, "Class, why don't you sing?" The class could not answer her. As the students left the room that day they felt a hatred and disgust for music.

Suppose Miss Perkins is an authentic, genuine person. She walks into the class and says, "Good morning, everybody. I am sorry, but I may be a little rattled and upset today. You see, a guy rammed into the back of my car on the way to school."

"Gosh! What happened?" the students ask excitedly. After a discussion of who he was and why and where it happened, the students feel they understand her problem. Because she shares her feelings with the class, Miss Perkins is able to relax. Then she and her class go on to a fruitful session, the time apparently lost in irrelevant talk having freed all of them for learning.

> Honest communication is the key to settle the undeclared wars that leave teacher and student angry, confused, or regretful.

Genuineness

A genuine person knows his inner feelings, keeps in touch with his emotional forces, and is courageous enough to share them with others. He does not hide behind a mask or engage in role behavior. He is true to himself and in his verbal and nonverbal behavior conveys a congruent message of who he is and what he feels and believes as well as what people can expect from him.

Although a genuine person "tells it like it is," he is careful not to babble indiscriminately about his private affairs. Prudence and tact prompt a teacher to shield the immature from the details of his own burdens or problems. Genuineness, however, demands that a

8

teacher disclose enough about his emotions and their causes to give the students security. Knowing that a teacher's upset is caused by conditions in his life, not by their activity, and that he is in control of himself, the students feel free to study and are able to learn.

For instance, a bandsman might say, "Please don't ask for reeds before class. You know how that annoys me. Can you wait until later?" Here the adult admits his weakness in being unable to tolerate some behavior. He shows his willingness to act as a human being and conveys to his students a feeling that they are free to be human, too. In his admission of feelings, the teacher has reduced the tension and threat which students experience when working with specialists in the field of music.

Students can trust a teacher who does not allow a buildup of frustration or boredom inside himself to cause an angry explosion. A nongenuine, maladjusted person can neither admit his feelings nor ventilate them, since he does not realize how anxious and annoyed he is. Further, the little he does know of himself he tries to hide in shame.[3] He works at this ceaselessly—twenty-four hours a day—and this hiding saps much of his energy. He knows that he feels uncomfortable, yet, instead of facing and eradicating his pain, unconsciously he passes it on to his class.

Although a teacher may try to hide behind a false front or cover his genuine self with a professional role, he betrays his true state through his gait, gestures, and speed of speech as well as through his tone of voice. Students easily assess a teacher's emotional framework within the first ten seconds of class.

One morning I was deeply engrossed in writing at a desk facing a wall. Some students came in for class. I heard them walk toward me, then stop. After some hesitation, Mary said, "Good morning." Without turning, I grumbled, "Hello." The students were puzzled at my behavior and asked, "Well, what's the matter? You mad or sick or something?"

I turned around and asked simply, "Why should I be mad or sick?"

"Well, I don't know," explained Julie. "Guess it was because you didn't greet us first, you didn't stop your work, and you didn't

9

seem to care about us. I suppose I just didn't feel welcome in here like I usually do.''

My preoccupation, so different from my usual warmth, frightened these freshmen. For the first half of class I could detect signs of fear. They believed my nonverbal behavior and continued to be perplexed about what it meant. Young people are threatened when they do not know the cause of a teacher's unusual behavior.

Is it good professional practice to admit one's personal feelings? Will the students think less of a teacher if he admits that he is nervous, concerned, frustrated, or bored? Experience proves otherwise. When youngsters find a genuine person who is not afraid of his negative feelings, they can more easily establish a rapport with him, because they can align their own human tendencies with his and find themselves equally human and equally acceptable. They can find new hope for themselves and learn that negative feelings as well as talents are qualities of a whole person who is precious and unique.

The honest, real teacher not only speaks and acts as he really feels; he is also usually able to respect and draw out the genuine uniqueness of his students. A real teacher meets others genuinely and does not treat them as things. One of the contributions of the great Martin Buber is his specifying of the two types of relationships, the ''I-It'' and the ''I-Thou'' encounter. The ''I-It'' relationship is that of a person meeting a thing. Educators who treat students as skill achievers and fact consumers actually depersonalize them and deal with them primarily as things. Music teachers who have rigid methods and use the same materials with all students are possibly guilty of an impersonal approach to teaching. Remarks such as ''I make my kids . . .'' or ''I don't care how they feel, I know . . .'' could betray an ''I-It'' relationship.[4]

In the ''I-Thou'' relationship, persons are in touch with their own personhood and mutually respect one another. Teachers who establish such a relationship contact the feelings of students and learn to estimate the unique needs of each student. They are willing at times to relinquish their plans made for the teaching period and allow students to direct their own educative procedures. Although they do not abandon their role as teachers, genuine educators are in close contact with the receptivity of the students as well as the educational needs of the situation.

Congruent communication and genuine behavior are an achievement for any teacher. One does not learn to "tell it like it is" without effort, rehearsing, and self-discipline. It is not just "doing what comes naturally." Realness demands practice, because it is a skill. It requires the artful selection of words and procedures. A genuine person is careful not to act artificially, but neither does he merely ramble on about anything that comes to his mind. Such careless talk disturbs and confuses students. It is only by sensitively watching student reaction to one's carefully chosen words that a teacher moves from phoniness to true communication.

Although genuineness is difficult to attain, it is the most crucial of all the means of rapport. Without genuineness no other qualities will really help; they will appear as mere tricks or shallow games. Since society at large is so engaged in game playing, teachers are apt to be caught up in fundamentally destructive ways of selling themselves and their product, music. Like their friends in other professions, music educators may be out of tune with their true personhood. Yet the struggle to overcome superficiality and deal genuinely with themselves and their students carries with it the rewards of becoming a truly great human being, one who can make a significant difference in the lives of young people.

An Out-of-Tune Music Teacher

"Do it again. Now, do it five times more!" shouts Mr. Kastor, his eyes fixed on the floor.

Susie, a high school junior, struggles through the flute cadenza again, missing even more notes this time. Her hands are perspiring, and her heart is filled with angry, put-down feelings. "Oh, if he only knew how he makes me feel like a child. How I wish he would let me figure this out myself. I'd like to feel it is my own cadenza."

"I've never heard such sloppy articulation! You should have heard how clearly Sally played this last year. You're just not trying!

Now, do it again!'' complains Mr. Kastor as he taps his finger on the music.

The worlds of Susie, a moderately talented but keenly sensitive teenager, and the achievement-oriented Mr. Kastor are extremely far apart. But an even sadder truth lies in the fact that the teacher is not interested in the world of beauty and pain within this lovely young girl. He does not care how she feels.

> We get too close to our music and too far from
> the reality the students live in.
>
> John Westmoreland

Empathy

Empathy, an essential condition for good rapport, is the teacher's inner experiencing of his student's struggle with himself and with his music. An empathic teacher can sense his student's inner world enough to piece it together and be supportive. He lends a willing ear to the feelings of anger, hostility, and suspicion which he knows will seriously hinder the student's achievement in music study. He can perceive anxiety and fear when a student perspires profusely or tenses his facial or body muscles. He notices rigidity early enough to prevent its destroying the success of the class session.

If the teacher knows the concerns and emotional stress of a student, he can plan an emotional release of these feelings. He can line up those feelings with suitable music or music activities through which the student can express himself. The extremes of register in both instrumental and vocal music can often satisfy the student's craving for power. Music with a driving beat and a ''go-go'' rhythm may captivate a bored student. Music with pulsating triplets can give the restless teenager a feeling of escaping on a moving vehicle. Music with heavy accents or great volume can give vent to feelings of hostility, anger, and rejection, which students so often experience. Using music that fulfills the emotional need of the student is a prime tool for fostering human growth as well as meaningful musical development.

Empathy is more than knowing and caring about a student's

feeling. When a teacher says, "I know how you feel," he is merely measuring what he thinks a student experiences and comparing it to what he has experienced himself. Because the teacher is not the student, he cannot really know just what the student feels. The effort of the really empathic teacher, however, is the attempt to, as the Indian says, "walk a mile in his moccasins." Unfortunately, most music educators fear even to look into the boots of their students. They are too busy and too afraid to get involved. They are content to keep their jobs and the approval of administrator and parents.

Empathy is sometimes difficult because students build walls around themselves. They try to remain opaque to adults. To crack through such a wall of protection is challenging for most teachers. Yet, because inwardly these students are crying out for love and acceptance, their needs are great. The teacher must find a point of connection with such a student. Usually there is one identifying point within a student which enables the two to share each other's experience. The teacher studies the youth; he seeks to find the unique inner rhythm within this person. There is an inner dynamism and harmonic system within each student upon which a teacher must play if he wishes to develop rapport. The teacher and student who are emotionally in tune with each other can then create meaningful music.

However, for the most part, empathy is not really taxing or difficult. An empathic teacher, in contact with his own feelings, notices the signals of strong feelings in his students and tries to take care of them. He allows the student to talk freely about him. He avoids being critical or judgmental. He refrains from advising and directing. He merely questions and stimulates the student, helping him to explore his true feelings, priorities, and growth needs. Together, student and teacher can engage in a deep sharing of goals and concerns.

> The helping role demands empathy not sympathy,
> information not advice and both support and
> reality factors instead of dependency relation-
> ships.[5]

When students experience feelings of disgust, anger, or disloyalty, they can do much harm. They can make serious errors and by expressing their negative feelings to others, can lower the morale of other students. Alert teachers approach such students and help them uncover their true feelings before they make hasty decisions.[6]

At other times students have general feelings or a confused mixture of feelings. They need help to trace them back to their specific causes. The following anecdote describes an example of this procedure.

Ken's face became very flushed whenever he was asked to play his trombone alone during band practice. Although he was the finest player in his section, he refused to practice his solo parts and played them poorly.

"Sorry," he would say. "Let someone else do it. I can't."

One day he became extremely embarrassed and angry. After class he told his teacher, "I hate the trombone. I can't play. I want to quit. Besides, I've got too much to do."

The teacher suspected that this outburst did not express Ken's basic feelings, because the boy showed much evidence of liking to play. The teacher motioned to a chair and said, "Sit down, Ken. I think we need to talk. You say you hate the trombone. Well, you don't seem to hate it all the time, do you? You seem to really enjoy playing except when you have a solo."

"Yeah, guess I really just hate solos," admitted Ken.

"Solos are not easy, are they, Ken?" asked the teacher in an assuring tone.

"Nah, but, well, solos aren't really all that bad. I seem to be able to play them at home. But, well, in school, it's different. Those silly girls always look around and embarrass me. I feel so stupid and silly. I just can't play."

As Ken mentioned the girls' influence on him, he seemed to become a little angry at himself for being so affected by them. As weeks went on, he began to realize that he really loved his trombone. He found it painful to play near the girls, but he gradually

14

solved his problem and made marked improvements in solo playing.

In the area of personal feelings, a teacher must approach the student with the utmost empathy and respect. A phrase which is highly empathic as well as nonthreatening is, "It must have felt . . ." The student usually feels safe in admitting his feelings when the teacher recognizes them without surprise. As the child or youth describes his highly subjective situation, the teacher can relate to it and put some kind of objective order into it. When a teacher is warm, accepting, and empathic, the channels of communication are easy to open.

When a young person is hurting, he wants someone who can share his pain. He wants to see his pain reflected, as in a mirror, in another person. He wants a mirror, not a sermon. A phrase such as "You shouldn't feel . . ." has a damaging effect on a student. He has a right to feel as he does. His emotions are part of his personhood.

Every human being, young or old, has both positive and negative feelings. He simply must know them and must deal with them intelligently and honestly. John Steinbeck writes of this in the book *East of Eden*:

> The greatest terror a child can have is that he is not loved, and rejection is the hell of fears. . . . And with rejecting comes anger, and with anger some kind of crime in revenge. One child, refused the love he craves, kicks the cat and hides his secret guilt; and another steals so that money will make him loved; and a third conquers the world—and always the guilt and revenge and more guilt.[7]

When trying to uncover feelings, a teacher should never argue against the student's experience. If a student says he is angry, a teacher accepts that without question. A student may be ambivalent—may have many other feelings seemingly more noticeable—but it is very harmful to confuse him with conflicting reports about his possible inner and exterior state. If the helper is to be a mirror, he must be open to the experience within the person as well as to his outer behavior. In order to bring peace to the restless and troubled, the teacher needs a large store of respect for every student.

Clarinet or Clarinetist?

"Sit down, David! Fix that spring yourself!" orders Mr. Whalen. "You're only trying to get attention." Ten-year-old David, feeling totally unaccepted, shuffles his way back to his chair in the third clarinet section.

"It must be nice," he mutters to himself, "to be rich enough to buy a clarinet that works. This darn thing . . . I wish my parents cared enough . . ."

As David tries to fix the spring, he quietly listens to Mr. Whalen's band. He watches Mr. Whalen as he drills the cut-off and works for better intonation.

What is this band really doing for David, sitting there rejected because of his poverty? For educators like Mr. Whalen, good instruments are more important than the little people who play them. David, who has an innate need for acceptance as well as an inborn talent for music, must look outside this music program for personal fulfillment.

> I feel the capacity to *care* is the thing that gives
> life its greatest significance and meaning.[8]

Warmth

The quality of warmth consists of a deep openness to and acceptance of the whole person of the student. This acceptance stems from a teacher's respect for what the person can become as well as what he already is.

Warmth is not sentimental, emotional, or immature. It has nothing to do with being "nice" in order to maintain a teaching position. It is not hypocritical or manipulatory.

A warm, understanding teacher prizes his student as an individual. He esteems him as a valuable person regardless of his particular behavior at the moment. A warm teacher cares for the student because the latter is valuable and has promise. Warm acceptance involves an open willingness for the student to have whatever feelings are real for him at the moment: hostility or tenderness, rebellion or submissiveness, assurance or self-deprecation. It means a kind of love for the student as he is and, finally it means a willingness to help him build his character in his own way.

I remember a student who followed my every assignment and suggestion slavishly. Noticing a certain compulsiveness in her behavior, I asked her why she was working so hard. Much to my amazement, the fourteen-year-old Phyllis broke out in tears and said, "My teacher last year said I was too dumb to learn." I was stunned. I wondered just what the teacher had really said. Although I questioned the idea that a teacher would have used those words, I had to admit that a teacher had in some way communicated a strong message of nonacceptance to this girl. Phyllis had so deeply internalized this teacher's rejection that even a year later she still felt the need to prove herself.

To be warm means to have an understanding heart. Understanding means to be able to "stand under" the level of problems and help a person at the source of his problem. When Phyllis spoke from her heart, then her voice was really the voice of the "I" of her essential personhood. Then, when I began to understand Phyllis at the level of my own essence, my "I-ness," even if only with my eyes, by quietly listening to her or by speaking a little phrase, she was able to feel that her burden of rejection had been shared and that she was no longer alienated and alone. Little by little she learned to believe in herself and her talents.

It seems that students are dwarfed in their attitudinal and maturational growth by negative feelings which they are afraid to express. Until they rid themselves of these notions and until they find courage and self-acceptance, they do not make progress as persons or as wholehearted musicians. Until they feel safe just being themselves, they cannot extend the frame of reference within which they perceive reality.

Experiences like these prove that music educators are capable of helping students make significant changes in their lives. But what about the students whom a teacher dislikes? Does the teacher dislike these persons, or does he dislike their behavior? Can he accept them although he disapproves of their behavior? Can he

17

separate their personal beings from their faulty patterns of fulfilling their needs? Does he subconsciously resent these students because they have faults which he, too, is trying to hide? Does he resent them because their faults are his as well? After such self-examination a teacher can attempt to deal with the student in a more respectful way—as a partner in the human condition. By focusing his attention on the integrity and respectability as well as potentiality of students and de-emphasizing their annoying behaviors, a teacher can learn to relate to students with warmth, acceptance and understanding.

> One neurotic has no eyes, many have no ears,
> others no heart or memory or legs to stand on.
> Most neurotic people have no center.[9]

Nonpossessive Caring

Mrs. Kling's desk was surrounded by her favorite students. Judy was there waiting to tell her that the altos did not get some notes. Jerry was ready to assure her that he would be willing to come for extra help. Karen was busy asking the easiest way to learn a certain passage.

"What lovely students!" mused Mrs. Kling. "How necessary and important I am to them!" Here was a teacher who prided herself on her students' dependence upon her and who relished the affection they poured on her. In focusing her attention upon the love she received from students rather than upon her own dedication to them, she revealed a possessive personality.

Possessiveness is more than overprotection. It tends to impose fixed life-patterns and values upon students. A possessive teacher can force his identity and ideals on a student. He cannot allow the student to think for himself. Possessiveness is a teacher's narrow love of self, a self-feeding device of a dwarfed personality. Unfortunately, the total effect of possessiveness in teachers is worse than the mere using of students to gain personal satisfaction. A possessive teacher cripples students by allowing them to depend on him rather than seek their own answers.

A nonpossessive teacher stimulates the powers within a student to ask questions and give fresh, revealing, and creative answers instead of those which are already in the teacher's head. He listens to new ideas. He is sufficiently brief in giving explanations. If he demonstrates for students, he does so only when he will not stifle their creativity in finding their own solutions. He refrains from taking credit for student work. He offers support when that is needed but is willing to let the student go when security is no longer necessary. Nonpossessive caring is simply a refined kind of love and respect for an autonomous human being.

> By cherishing and holding the child in absolute esteem, the teacher is establishing an environmental climate that facilitates growth and becoming.[10]

Nonmanipulative Respect

When a teacher accepts a student, he accepts the whole human being. He feels an unconditional positive regard for the whole person. He sees the student as worthy of esteem. A teacher fails in respect when he judges, uses, or manipulates students.

Yet, accepting a student does not mean condoning bad behavior. This would mean that by approving the person a teacher dwarfs his future growth. Certainly, students need change. Teachers accept them as candidates for change. By their nonmanipulative prizing of students, teachers stimulate constructive change and development in students.

Why do teachers fail in respecting the inherent dignity of their students? Why do educators push students around as things? Here are some reasons: (1) There are too many extra-musical responsibilities. If they are to survive as paid teachers, they must produce adequately. (2) Teachers are sensitive to "bad" sounds and sometimes respond harshly when they hear displeasing sounds. (3) Sometimes teachers think of music as a digital skill. The slower the fingers, the poorer the person. (4) Keyboard teachers, especially, can become fixed in a method which they force on all students because it simplifies their work. (5) Teacher reputation is of such high priority that some project the blame for failure on the student. Johnny simply is not talented. (6) Time and efficiency are of prime value. Students' feelings and goals are caught in the crunch.

The list is endless. In the rush and shuffle of music activities, human beings can be disrespected and manipulated. Often the pleasant, congenial personality of the teacher can cover up this basic distortion of human values. At other times students decry the sham and phoniness of teachers who use the performance of others to build a good reputation.

> . . . A teacher who is harsh and unsympathetic may interfere with the process of healthy development. In such an atmosphere the child can no longer be his forthright self, free to inquire and to develop. Instead, he must defend himself. Even the strongest beginner . . . cannot be completely immune to the humiliation that may be inflicted on him by a sarcastic, punitive teacher.[11]

Dealing with Conflict

At no time do students have such "pushed-around" feelings as when they are publicly blamed. During times of conflict, a teacher is often tempted to be disrespectful and downright uncivil toward students. Mr. Shift, for instance, projects his angers and problems on the students by saying, "You are lazy," when it is really his procedures which are more to blame because they are not appealing enough to catch student interest. He says, "You are not concentrating and are being very careless," when he finds himself fragmented. He thinks that good professional practice demands that he never admit mistakes. Instead of facing the fact that his methods are ineffective and his materials are not relevant to students, he looks at his class (who are squirming because of the tense atmosphere) and shouts, "You stupid fools! Why don't you ever pay attention?"

A teacher is at his worst when he not only denies his own feelings, but projects his problems on the student.[12] The "you are" statements directed at the student are disturbing and hurtful. They can do lasting damage to a student's self-image. They deny the student's perception and feelings; they argue with his feelings. They downgrade the student's tastes, opinions, and personality.

At times of conflict a genuine and respectful person will tell a class how he honestly feels. If he is irritated or furious, he says just that—in a nonthreatening but forceful way. Instead of projecting blame on students, a genuine person will say simply, "I'm feeling angry and disgusted. Now, let's work together." A teacher who constantly projects the blame for distressing situations on the members of his class can do them irreparable harm. In contrast, a genuine and respectful teacher clears the air during times of conflict with a brief, laconic statement geared to the situation. He admits the truth of his feelings and attacks the problem, not the students.[13]

On a hot and humid summer day my junior band members were uncomfortable in their small rehearsal room. Then, while I was helping the clarinetists with a trill, Ralph, a drummer, gave vent to his restless, unhappy feelings. He began throwing his drumsticks into the air and twirling them as if they were batons. Just as I turned around, Ralph's drumstick hit and broke a window. Because I, too, was suffering from the heat, I was ready to lose my temper. Then I noticed the pain in Ralph's face. The accident itself was not his problem. His distress was the same as mine; we were all frustrated. I said, simply, "Well, Ralph, pick up the pieces. We must take care of that glass." Ralph felt relieved that I did not publicly punish him. He also learned that day that there are safer ways of relieving tension and boredom during rehearsals.

Students can show their objection to being "shoved around" by behaving in a sassy, critical, or rebellious manner. They are not merely "trying to get attention." They are subconsciously reacting to an unhealthy condition in the teacher and the atmosphere of the class. Because of their sensitivity to discourteous treatment, students who tend to misbehave seem to become even more demonic when the manipulative efforts of a teacher irritate them.

Teachers who respect the child deal with misbehavior by probing the emotional motivation behind the act. During the class a teacher

21

speaks firmly but in a nonthreatening tone: "I don't like it when people speak to me this way." Later, a misbehaving student receives the kind of attention which will really help him. The teacher sees him privately and tries to uncover the feelings which led to the scene. A mature adult can respect a sassy child and often can evoke a positive response from him.

Esteem for Particular Students

It is extremely important for the teacher to consider and evaluate what he thinks of each student as a person. Mr. Bond, who introduces a student saying, "This is—ah-ah-er—second alto—what is your name?" demonstrates a tendency to think of students as things, not people. Certainly, it is no accident that Mr. Bond does not know the names of his singers. Frankly, he does not know them as people. He thinks of them as performers, not as unique human beings.

When a teacher has low esteem for a student, his manner and actions betray his attitude even when his thoughts remain unspoken. Interior labeling of students with negative evaluations such as "untalented," "unreliable," "slow learner" has a devastating effect on a student. Although these thoughts remain unspoken in the classroom or studio, students know and feel these judgments. Because they sense these mental assessments of their potential, students are subconsciously prevented from growing. With this internal labeling the teacher keeps the students in the psychological state of feeling inferior.

> The tragedy of [bad] . . . "communication" lies not in the lack of love, but in the lack of respect; not in the lack of intelligence, but in the lack of skill.[14]

Skills of Rapport

In order to build and increase his ability to relate to students and meet their needs more effectively, a teacher uses certain skills or techniques. With the skills of listening, noticing, and interpreting nonverbal behavior and classroom reactions, a teacher strengthens his rapport with his students.

Listening

Listening, the art of evaluating verbal and nonverbal behavior, is one of the most essential skills of establishing rapport. Like any other skill, the technique of listening is learned behavior. Because people feel the need to send and receive messages, they must develop some degree of listening skills. When a teacher feels a greater need to obtain feedback from his students, he can develop a higher level of listening skill.

People develop fixed patterns of communicating messages and deciphering the meaning of a sender's message. The subtle aspect of sending messages lies in the fact that a speaker subconsciously uses body language when trying to convey a verbal message. Further complexity results from the listener's subconscious reaction to these signs.

Since there is often a conflict between what a person is saying and what he is acting out with his body, a careful observer notes both body language and spoken words. There is a split in the message of the sender when he says one thing which he thinks is proper and feels a quite different message which he is afraid to convey. The diagram illustrates the complexity of the listening process. Notice that not only is there a split in the message of the sender; the listener, too, has many choices and many factors to consider.

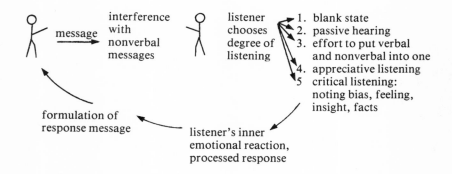

This example may clarify the meaning of the diagram. Nancy is telling her teacher that she is sorry she missed choir practice because her bus was late. Her face, however, is lit with a playful smile; her nonverbal message is that of mischief rather than of guilt or sorrow. The teacher chooses the third level of listening, adds the opposing data, and responds by asking a more specific question. He does not believe the verbal message.

Usually a person has a rather fixed way of listening and fluctuates only slightly from it.[15] However, when a listener is more interested or feels more love and care, he will exert more energy in his listening response.

Noting Nonverbal Behavior

As the diagram shows, the interference of a person's body language can completely destroy a verbal message. A highly perceptive listener is able to sort out the elements of his reaction. What is the verbal message? What is the "feeling" message that the person's sign language is conveying?

Experts believe that eighty percent of all communication is nonverbal.[16] By this they mean that when body language such as fumbling, fidgeting, and stiffness are interfering with a spoken message of assurance, for example, the listener believes, not the words, but the nonverbal meaning of the body's behavior. When a teacher's voice is pinched with tension, no student will believe his words of hope. Students take the message they feel is more honest.

It is easier to notice behavior, however, than it is to correctly interpret behavioral signs. For instance, Frank may appear tense when he is merely cold. Susie's hands may be trembling but her feelings are quite courageous. Linda may be overactive before the concert, but she is more excited than apprehensive. The teacher with good rapport will reach out to the student and test his observations and hunches before drawing conclusions about the student's real feelings.

Noting Group Reactions during Teaching

During the first few moments of class a perceptive teacher surveys the mood and spirit of the group. Very noticeable feelings such as group nosiness, sulkiness, or boredom may demand a change of procedure for the class.

One natural reaction for the teacher in such a situation is to become interiorly upset and to turn on his charm and showmanship exteriorly. Reverting to flashy "fun" music could be the option of the teacher whose main objective is to maintain order. Older children and teenagers, however, resent childish experiences and are usually eager for an engrossing experience. They crave a teacher who is direct and effective, and who keeps the class moving even though the materials may be challenging. When a teacher senses that the emotions of the class are extremely high or low, his best approach is to avoid talking, give only short, precise directions, and keep the students' minds and muscles working. Emotional power channeled into learning takes the students far.

As the class goes on, the teacher keeps in touch with how the students are reacting. Young people who have been confined to a classroom for most of their lives create an adequate signaling system. They toy with keys and clothes; they glance at the clock; they slouch; they wrinkle their brows, and, above all, they misbehave. Teachers who watch signals and respond to them by using appropriate relational and pedagogical techniques will not usually waste class time because students are lost, discouraged, bewildered, or bored.

> The only reason to live is to grow—therefore
> growth is worth any price.[17]

The Risk of Establishing Rapport

For various reasons, music educators may be reluctant to work at establishing a good rapport, at approaching their profession humanistically. First, music can easily be reduced to a science and subdivided into behavior units. A scientific teacher goes into a class, merely demonstrates a behavior, and waits for the students to imitate and master the skill. If he is successful, the teacher can boast that the students have learned "music" in his class. Such a teacher, too afraid to deal with either the art of music or the humanity of his students, will not take the risk of trying to establish rapport. When his students demonstrate music behaviors, he believes his teaching is adequate.

Other teachers are reluctant to humanize their approach to teaching because of the pressures and deadlines caused by their orientation toward performance in music education. They fear that the quality of their performance will deteriorate if they shift their focus away from producing superior work. For such teachers, stopping to smile at Ann or to compliment George wastes time which is badly needed to drill fingers, embouchures, and breathing organs. The deadline of performing appearances is more real to such teachers than the human beings in front of them.

A third factor which militates against the establishment of rapport is the size of performing groups and classes in schools. These groups are sometimes so large that teachers simply cannot keep in human contact with students. One might be able to trace a vicious circle of cause and effect in this situation by noting the factors in the following diagram:

26

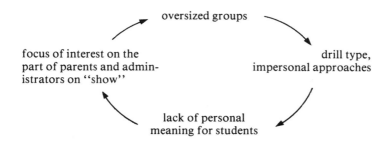

oversized groups

focus of interest on the
part of parents and admin-
istrators on "show"

drill type,
impersonal approaches

lack of personal
meaning for students

Although a change in this situation seems imperative, a radical shift toward a more humanistic approach to music education will not come for many years.[18] However, as humanistic education gains wider acceptance in other areas, music educators, too, will gradually begin to take the risk of becoming more human in their approach.

Rapport is work, discipline; it does not come spontaneously. Being true to others is just as difficult as being true to oneself. However, the simplest step in the right direction will lead to the next. Taking risks and experimenting with the various means of rapport slowly brings success and satisfaction to the teacher. It is by relating that one creates a pattern of relating. By being truly alert and alive one becomes responsive to very alive young people.

One cannot say too often that teaching human beings is risky. There are no guarantees or set paths. There is no one-to-one correlation between "good" approaches to students and "good" reactions from them. There is no complete assurance that students will respond positively when a teacher attempts to show his care and concern for them. Since dealing with George, the power-hungry boy, is quite different from dealing with nervous Allen, a teacher can blunder badly and make mistakes in his early attempts to establish rapport. Because both teachers and students differ widely, there are no definite procedures in human relations. Each human experience is new and creative.

Although changing one's attitude toward students as well as toward music is a risk, there are many rewards for the brave teacher. Average students relax when teachers are human beings who do not hide in their aura as specialists and authorities. Hostilities disappear in an atmosphere of kind and human control. Students tend to develop trust in and respect for a teacher who considers them worthy persons who can handle freedom responsibly.

"Yes, that sounds good. But do students really learn when rapport exists?" a teacher may ask. Research has shown that students learn better when they are treated as people who are becoming responsible for their own education.[19] A teacher who does not merely "show and tell," but facilitates the students' own investigation of music, will probably experience more thrilling and more lasting success. Among our own experiences as young students, we remember and treasure those instances of learning when we were completely involved. Since good rapport reduced threat and hostility factors in us and made us feel like more worthy persons, we were able to absorb musical learning and enjoy artistic, creative experiences.

A continuous struggle to find new ways of reaching students is common to all dedicated teachers. David Thatcher puts it this way:

> A child learns, a child doesn't learn, and I, as a teacher, learn to live with mystery. If I can live comfortably with mystery, I can relax more often in the classroom. If I can relax, students can more easily relax and learn.

> It is precisely because we teachers set our sights so low and risk so little that we accomplish so little. To teach, I risk, I dare, I often lose, but when I win, I win something that is worth the effort and the risk—I help a person win himself.[20]

The risk of achieving rapport with students is well worth taking. A risk is a growth experience. It gives new insight and understanding which will enable future teaching to be more meaningful and significant. If today's risk seems to be a flop, it still has much value for the teacher. A risk readies a teacher for more successful educational projects in the future.

All of music study involves risk. Investing hours, months, and years of practice as well as thousands of dollars for a questionable career is risky business. Yet it pays off. So, too, a teacher who begins the practice of communication and develops the skills of rapport becomes a competent and successful educator after much practice and effort. Like the virtuoso violinist who plays as though the problems of fingering, bowing, and double stopping never existed, the educator who takes the risk of teaching with rapport becomes able to facilitate growth in others naturally and effectively.

Notes

1. Haim G. Ginott, *Between Parent and Child* (New York: Avon Books, 1965), p. 47.

2. Carl R. Rogers, "Two Divergent Trends," *Existential Psychology,* ed. Rollo May (New York: Random House, 1961), p. 93.

3. Sidney M. Jourard, *The Transparent Self (New York: D. Van Nostrand Co., 1964),* p. 26.

4. Martin Buber, *I and Thou* (New York: Charles Scribner's Sons, 1958).

5. Walter M. Lifton, *Working with Groups* (New York: Avon Books, 1965), p. 106.

6. Haim G. Ginott, *Between Parent and Child,* pp. 30-40.
1965), p. 40.

7. John Steinbeck, *East of Eden* (New York: Viking Press, 1952), pp. 170-71.

8. Pablo Casals, "Life: A Fantasy with Music," in *They Talk About Music,* ed. Robert Cumming, vol. I (New York: Belwin/Mills Publishing Corp., 1971), p. 46.

9. Frederick Perls, *In and Out the Garbage Pail* (New York: Bantam Books, Inc., 1969), p. 140.

10. Clark Moustakas, *The Authentic Teacher* (Cambridge, Mass.: Doyle Publishing Co., 1966), p. 13.

11. Arthur T. Jersild, *In Search of Self* (New York: Teachers College Press, Columbia University, 1952), p. 94.

12. Haim G. Ginott, *Between Teacher and Child* (New York: Congruent Communications, 1972), p. 83.

13. *Ibid.,* p. 72.

14. Haim G. Ginott, *Between Parent and Child,* p. 25.

15. Larry L. Barker, *Listening Behavior* (Englewood Cliffs, N.J.: Prentice-Hall, 1971), p. xvii.

16. James J. Thompson, *Beyond Words* (New York: Scholastic Magazines, Citation Press, 1973), p. 1.

17. Robert R. Carkhuff, *Belly to Belly Back to Back* (Amherst, Mass.: Human Resource Development Press, 1971), p. 79.

18. Robert H. Klotman, *The School Music Administrator and Supervisor: Catalyst for Change in Music Education* (Englewood Cliffs, N.J.: Prentice-Hall, 1973), p. 135.

19. David N. Aspy, *Toward a Technology for Humanizing Education* (Champaign, Ill.: Research Press Company, 1972), p. 17.

20. David Thatcher, *Teaching, Loving and Self-Directed Learning* (Pacific Palisades, Calif.: Goodyear Publishing Company, 1973), p. 34, 36.

Knowing and Utilizing Personal Emotions

How a person feels is more important than what he knows.

Earl C. Kelley

Knowing Our Relational Stance

Fundamental to the art of teaching with rapport is the teacher's realization of his personal stance in relating. Only after a teacher knows his feelings about himself, his life position in relating, and why he wants to relate to others, can he deal with people successfully.

Then, too, after a teacher confronts himself, he finds new inner forces which can be utilized in driving lessons home to students. Even his negative energies, such as anger, anxiety, and fear, can be channeled into positive teaching power and success. Once a teacher knows himself he can begin to relate.

The teacher, however, does not start to relate on his first day of teaching. Relationships begin in early infancy. A short study of how relationships grow may clarify the process of relating.

When Do We Learn to Relate?

Some psychologists believe that a baby can feel his mother's acceptance or rejection of him even before he is born. After birth the child steadily gains greater ability to relate as he plays with his toys and interacts with his family. With his cries and physical motions a baby communicates his needs and wants as well as his messages of anger, loneliness, hunger or pain. As the little one begins to realize that he does not control things, he discovers that he must relate to others in order to be happy and satisfied.

The small child knows and values only his own experience. He possesses a simple but consistent value system which, however, creates relational problems for him. An inner power prompts him to say, in the words of the song, "I want what I want when I want it!" Although he feels that his whole personal value system is more real, more wise, and more important to him than any other standard, he receives severe criticism of his inner valuing processes. Adult admonitions make no sense to him. Yet the sting of verbal or physical punishment convinces him that he must conform, at least at times. Barry Stevens puts it this way:

> In the beginning, I was one person, knowing nothing but my own experience. Then I was told things, and I became two people. . . . In the beginning was I, and I was good. Then came other I. Outside authority. This was confusing.[1]

The child then goes into a stage where he shifts from following his own inner values at one time and obeying authority at another. An example of this alternation between relating to self and relating to parent is this incident.

Lisa, twenty-one months, saw eggs on the table while Mother was talking on the phone. She felt the urge to be like Mother. But she also felt the internalization of Mother's "No! No!" warnings of previous occasions. She found it hard to balance these two opposing forces. Upon arriving back, Mother found Lisa breaking the eggs on the floor while shaking her head and muttering, "Mama says, 'Mustn't!' Mama says, 'Mustn't!' "

Life Position or Relational Stance

At about the age of two of the toddler establishes a position or stance in his relating patterns. Usually a child takes the inferiority stance. Since he is smaller, less powerful, and less developed in every way than the adults around him, he makes a most serious judgment: "I'm not as good as you."

This statement of surrender on the part of the child is so deliberate and so forceful that it simplifies all of his relating experiences. The conviction that he is inferior becomes a firm and consistent relational standard. Because it is adopted in early childhood and is highly reinforced, the inferiority stance continues to be the life position for most adults throughout their lives.*

It is quite safe to say that most teachers and almost all students relate as though they were inferior to the person they deal with. They have a "less than" feeling which they have carried with them since they were about two years old. Because of this, the people involved in music education settings tend to down-play the value of what Carl Rogers calls their inner "organismic basis for valuing."[2] They tend to discount the validity of their personal judgments. They also readily give in to unthinking conformity in order to gain acceptance, a sense of belonging, or a feeling of importance.

Mr. Shift, for instance, who projects his inability to manage a choir on the students themselves, is actually trying to hide from his inferiority feelings. Because of a strong need to compensate for his feelings of unworthiness, he makes unrealistically high demands on his choir. Although his students sing quite well, they may sustain lasting personal hurts from associations with Mr. Shift. What has

---

* Opinion of Harry Stack Sullivan taken from G. S. Blum, *Psychoanalytic Theories of Personality* (New York: McGraw-Hill, 1953), pp. 73-74.

gone wrong? Mr. Shift himself is a talented, highly educated musician working with gifted singers. Can he adjust his relating habits? Can he replace his negative, inferior view of himself with a positive stance in tune with reality? Certainly. He can find the source of his anxiety, meet it, and channel his energies into positive teaching power.

> Society is not organized to free man's creative potential but rather to maintain him with minimal potency. It frees man's little finger only rather than both of his whole hands for creative activities, whether tangible or interpersonal.[3]

Effects of Culturation

It is not only because of a teacher's inferiority complex that he relates as a person alienated from his true inner being. The pressures of society may also effectively prevent a person's choosing what his inner experiences prefer. From the time of birth each individual feels punished by society for indulging in free and spontaneous choices which, though they are good in themselves, are considered forbidden behaviors. Social pressures sanction and reward conformity. Cultural forces lead to wearing hats, playing games, and hiding behind excuses and facades. Little by little such behaviors become a way of life for many people.

Because of this, teachers may find themselves in deep relational trouble. Culture rewards them for being nongenuine. Society considers people to be noble and worthy when they are mainly liars and sham conformers to social mores. Individuals who abandon the wisdom of their own inner personal value processes are said to be serving a common good. Those who repress their feelings and are alienated from their own personhood are considered good citizens. Is it any wonder that teachers have problems in rapport, that they are often characterized by an inner emptiness or hollowness?

It is ten long minutes before junior band rehearsal will be over and Bill Terrior, a young, but bored, director, is looking for a "fun" way to end the class.

"OK, kids, before you go, I'm going to show you a new saxophone which just arrived," he announces with sudden enthusiasm.

"Wow! Ain't she a beaut!" exclaims Greg as he sees the instrument. The students crowd around the director as he demonstrates its features.

After wetting the reed, Bill begins to dazzle his class with a few showy cadenzas. He plays some of his favorite pieces.

"Gosh, can he ever play fast!" "Oh, such high notes!" "How can he hold his breath so long?" whisper the students while he plays. When he finally stops they tell him, "You're the best player we ever saw."

"Yeah, I play a little. Thanks. But when I was in college I won . . ." Bill continues nostalgically. As he talks on and on about his student life as a young artist, he thinks of how different life was then. People applauded his rare virtuosity. Now no one seems to notice him. Then he was somebody. What is he now?

As he relates his honors and prizes, the boys and girls lose interest, put away their instruments, and leave. Alex, the drummer, takes a stick and beats away at the drum fiercely.

"OK, Alex, run along. Goodbye," says Mr. Terrior, hiding behind a false smile. He would deny that he dislikes Alex. He finds it necessary to keep telling himself constantly that he likes the boy for his talent, energy, and resourcefulness. As Alex leaves, Mr. Terrior represses bothersome questions such as "Why did Alex beat on the drum? What was he really saying?"

As he glances around the room, he sees Susie's flute music lying on the floor. It bears the footprints of several thoughtless students. Rather than honestly admit his frustration over carelessness, however, he avoids that discomfort and muses, "I'm glad I saved her music before the janitor got here."

It is now the end of the day. As Bill puts on his jacket, he looks at its lapels, which are studded with the pins of fraternal organizations. Bill is a do-gooder, a kind and generous person.

Yet, Bill Terrior is a phony, hollow man. He shows his superiority in order to be prized by his students. With his rationalization, denial, repression of feelings and boasting he thinks he is presenting himself as a truly great person. In reality he is fooling only himself.

What can Bill do to help himself? By facing and accepting his feelings and needs, he can satisfy his cravings in an adult way. He can admit honestly to a friend, "I need encouragement and support." After gaining a feeling of worthiness and reinforced confidence in himself, he can admit and master his emotions and approach his class in a more genuine way.

Facing the Self

Why would Bill Terrior deny that Alex makes him angry? Why does he waste class time trying to win his students' praise? Why does he deny his feelings? Bill is shielding himself from reality because he has fixed an ideal image of himself; and he blocks out, filters out, and distorts any information which contradicts the ideal self he thinks he is. He admits only to those emotions or motivations which reinforce that ideal self.

A man who pretends to be "nice" and accepting when he is really angry actually dehumanizes himself. He wants to be a god, an exemplar, rather than a warm, real man. If teaching were to require an infringement on personal identity, that is, if this calling demanded that a person be out of tune with himself, it would be a demeaning profession. On the contrary, the teacher need not choose to be someone he is not. His deepest responsibility is not to help others play or enjoy music; his highest natural duty is to be himself and to be open to his own experiences.[4]

A person who wishes to solve the problem of alienation can revitalize his real, genuine self by becoming alert and aware of himself and his reactions. When he does this, he may find, to his horror, a dislike and disgust for his real self. He may shrink from self-knowledge and feel an urgent need to hide behind excuses and facades. He may find that he pretends, quarrels, boasts, and lies. He may discover that he does not really fulfill his deep needs for security, love, and self-actualization.

His problem, however, lies not only in the pain of such self-confrontation. A teacher finds himself caught up in the hurried pace of teaching. Life as a teacher demands quick, simple patterns coping with problems. He runs to teach, runs out to lunch, runs back to write out some parts and falls into his chair at night too exhausted to think deeply. Such a way of life may indicate that he has not ranked his priorities. Should he rise above the level of being just a people-pleaser? Should he prefer to become an open, aware, and fully functioning human being? Should he place his personal priorities in self-fulfillment or should he continue to seek the ego satisfaction attained by living in accordance with others' expectations?

Awareness of self is a slowly evolving, unfolding process.[5] Little by little an aware person drops his facades and defense mechanisms and dares to be open to his own experience. With growing awareness comes the ability to know greater possibilities for choosing a richer life as well as the strength to deal with emotional highs and lows. When a man begins to face himself and his feelings, his success in relating to students grows. As he chooses more self-enhancing behaviors, his professional success provides him with further rewards.

> You tell yourself that you are weak and you hate
> yourself for it. The truth is that you are weak and
> so am I. And it's not such a terrible thing![6]

Readiness for Change

What prompts a teacher to think he needs change? Often it is an acute problem in his teaching. When student morale runs low, when parents withdraw their support, or when classes become chaotic, the anxious teacher must look for ways to change. At other times inner distress, unrest, emptiness, or discouragement can prompt a teacher to admit, "There must be a better way to live."

When a teacher notices that his personal problems and lack of rapport are alienating others, his new insight into his need for help is a first major step in removing his problems. Next he must seek help and courageously share his deep feelings. A definite and specific plan for improvement is a final step in personality correction.[7]

How may this sequence of steps in personal growth be initiated? Suppose Miss Perkins runs into the faculty room after an unsuccessful class. There she finds her friend Judy and begins to tell her about the whole series of unfortunate happenings—her car accident; endless detail about her restless, rebellious class. As she finishes, she breaks down in tears, sobbing, "Judy, I don't know why I'm such a failure!"

Judy listens to her empathically. "You're really down, Carrie. It seems as if everything went wrong, huh?" she says gently.

Now Carrie feels free to go on telling exactly how she is feeling inside. Through her empathy Judy makes Carrie's emotional upset quite objective. By clarifying exactly how Carrie feels, Judy helps her friend begin to understand herself. Little by little Carrie sees her personal and professional problems more clearly and begins to believe that she can overcome them.

Carrie needs hours of heart-to-heart talk with some supportive friend whom she really trusts. Although she may feel a need for change and a desire for new behaviors, she continues to be threatened by the risk and pain involved in shifting her attitudes and values. She fears confrontation and criticism. Carrie cringes from the stark honesty with which she must reval her feelings. Yet when she acquires insight into her methods of wearing masks, playing games, and using defense mechanisms, she gains a refreshing impetus for personal change. By adopting realistic plans for self-growth, she gains in personal enrichment and in new hope for her teaching career.

> I don't want to conquer, save the world . . . I just
> want to see my part of it clear.
>
> Bronson

Self-Disclosure

Maybe the reason why many music educators have relational problems is that they are "loners." They often work alone. In large schools where there are many teachers, they often find themselves competing with each other. These conditions hinder the likelihood that teachers will feel the freedom or the trust to confide in others and experience mutual growth.

Although music education situations often do not seem conducive to it, the disclosure of personal feelings and problems is a powerful and necessary means to maturity as well as to success in teaching. When a teacher verbalizes and admits his emotions to an accepting person, his hazy notions and feelings become objective material upon which he can take action. Often when an individual says, "I'm angry! I'm jealous!" the feelings subside and reason regains mastery.

It may come as a surprise to music educators, who usually work by themselves and relate deeply with only a very few people, that personal growth takes place better when two or more people interact with one another.[8] When an individual opens himself honestly to another and spills out just what is deepest in his heart, he can come in contact with himself for the first time. He is able to experience the feelings, desires, attitudes, and goals which form the basis of the "I" that is the core of his being. Why this insight and understanding of oneself comes from self-disclosure to another person is a mystery.[9] However, it is in speaking about his true self that one finds the "raw materials" of his personhood. With these raw materials objectified by exposure, the problem of identity dissolves. "That which is expressed is impressed," as Aristotle puts it. When a man hears his own voice revealing truths, he begins to believe his true personhood.

Certain problems, such as students' quitting lessons, can cause a feeling of rejection in a teacher and can initiate a certain degree of self-examination. Because he feels judged, a teacher may want to "blow up" to someone. Although the situation could lead to self-confrontation, which, in turn, would foster personal and professional growth, a teacher could fail to face himself honestly and, instead, hide behind excuses and defenses. One teacher might say falsely, "Mark quit and I'm glad he's gone." Another might rationalize, "I'm glad Mark quit, although he was a good player. Now his sister can have the instrument." Another might project the blame on others by complaining, "Yeah, who can have any success with this setup around here?" Still another may deny that Mark's leaving was a loss to him. Such teachers have not only lost a student. They have missed a chance to learn and improve themselves as well as forestall further losses to their music programs.

On the contrary, Mark's teacher can confide honestly, "Gee, Sam, I feel discouraged. I lost another student—a good one, too. Where did I go wrong? What is it that I am not seeing?" This teacher, through careful analysis and self-disclosure to another person, can improve himself and his rapport with students and thereby lower the mortality rate in his performing units.

Little by little, as an individual reports his feelings and reactions to situations honestly and completely to a friend, his self-alienation is transformed into self-realization. He comes out from behind the curtain of protectiveness and sees himself clearly. In the presence of an accepting person a man can dare to see and express his feelings, impulses, memories, capacities, and dreams about his destiny and the possibility of personal fulfillment. Encouraged by a warm friend, he can acquire the courage to be himself, the strength to claim both his limitations and his talents and to recognize them as legitimate parts of himself. After discovering this balance between his weaknesses and his powers, he genuinely loves and accepts every part of himself.

Musicians are often obsessed with the desire to become uniquely creative, inspirational, and artistic people. Wrapped up in the ecstasy and rapture of musical expression, they can use music as an escape from reality. Yet the person who is brave enough to know himself and becomes a master of his feelings and behavior is more free to put his fully realized self into his musical expression and his teaching activities.

> We consist only of our experience. All one knows of himself, and all one can value, is his own consciousness. The most important thing possible— is the quality of that consciousness. The ultimate goal of all education is to improve that quality.[10]

BASIC NEEDS AND MOTIVATIONS OF ALL PEOPLE

As a person discloses his feelings and inner urges to another person, he reveals a deeper level of himself, that of needs and motivations. Feelings are surface indicators of needs. In fact, the habitual behavior patterns which a person adopts to meet his basic needs form the essence of his personality.[11]

A need is an "inner electro-chemical process"[12] which prompts a person to think or act. Psychologists who have studied the patterns which people develop in meeting needs have found that basically all men fulfill their needs according to a sequence. There is an irreversible progression of needs extending from lower needs of the body to the higher needs of the mind and soul. Abraham Maslow formed a ladder of needs[13] as well as a comprehensive theory of motivation which is helpful in understanding the "why" of all human behavior and also the motivational states of individuals.

Although many people seem quite irrational in the choices they make, they actually follow a sequence in meeting needs. A person climbs the "ladder," meeting the lower needs first. When he has satisfied lower needs, he then feels the urge to satisfy higher needs.[14] Therefore, a musician will not ordinarily be prompted to satisfy his aesthetic needs when he has nagging needs for love, security, or even for food and rest.

MASLOW'S LADDER OF NEEDS

6: Cognitive, rational needs

Need to know and understand: curiosity exploration; need to systematize, organize, analyze, seek relationships.

5: Self-Actualization

Integrity needs: creative personality fulfillment, vision, expression, communication, sharing, courage, conviction, need for others' support.

4: Ego Needs

Self-esteem and reputation: confidence, achievement, competence, reputation, status, strength, usefulness.

3: Love and Belonging

Close, intimate relationship with significant others; self-disclosure and deep communication; love, trust, allowing for support and confrontation.

2: Safety, Security Needs

Security from want: home, money, job, aesthetic needs. Security from oppression: personal and professional rejection. Security from fear: failure, personal, domestic, professional dependence.

1: Physiological Needs

Health, food, sleep, exercise, leisure, sex.

Examples of Meeting Needs

The most basic needs are physical. A teacher is in close contact with his needs for rest, food, and a sense of biological well-being. His pain, discomfort, and weariness become very effective motivators in choice making. He may find that he is an irritable teacher when he has a toothache or a pinched toe, because he is denying his need for physical comfort. Such a teacher is somewhat unready to meet his higher needs or those of others until he satisfies his physical and biological needs.

The second need, security, is a most sensitive and comprehensive need. To be secure means to feel safe and protected. It means to be free of fear, anxiety, and oppression. Security denotes a certain kind of stability and assurance of status. Job security is a great worry for many educators. When a director is insecure in his job, he tends to be more manipulative than personal in his relations with others. His discipline, his choice of materials, and his personal demeanor reveal an insecurity which undermines his effectiveness in directing his musical activities. By facing insecurity and aiming at small goals which bring instant success, a young or unstable person can solidify his status.

In society today the tendency to escalate to higher positions creates a whole hierarchy of insecure people. Men and women often climb to positions of power until they reach a level at which they are incompetent and insecure. Because status and honor are so desperately needed by attention-craving, insecure individuals, there are many key positions in music education settings which are being held by moderately capable persons. Such educators focus their attention to a great extent on retaining their positions and fooling others into believing that they are adequate.

This puts a ceiling on progress in music education. The man on top often cannot really risk experimenting. He hesitates in changing or improving music programs because of his insecurity. Instead of being an inspiring or progressive leader, he feels the need, at times, to act out his role in inhuman ways. Such music education leaders are sometimes highly competitive, hostile, insensitive, manipulatory, or subtly tyrannical. By admitting their limitations and meeting their needs to be relatively secure professionally, such educators could accept positions which they could handle and become, thereby, happier, more effective persons.

The third need is for love and belonging. When a man feels safe, he begins to crave the love, trust, and acceptance of other people. He feels a strong need to belong, in a close and important way, to his family, his organization, and his students. He feels a need to be "counted in" with a good degree of warmth. If he is to function adequately, he needs emotional support—acceptance and affection—from his colleagues.

There are, unfortunately, unhealthy ways of meeting the need for love. Often a man will deny he has this need and will subconsciously feed his craving for acceptance by using immature psychological devices. One person will cling to his students, making satellites of them. Another will try to get attention and pseudo satisfaction by showing off or bragging. Still another will downplay his work and thus provoke others to assure him of his worth.

The fourth need is self-esteem and a good reputation among associates. The teacher needs to feel that he is a valuable person doing well in his life and profession; he needs to see himself as a good teacher and worthy person. Release from this need allows him a certain freedom to be genuine, empathic, and accepting. A teacher who highly esteems himself has the ego strength to take the risks of establishing rapport. Because high assessment leads to more positive thinking and higher achievement, a cycle of cause and effect results:

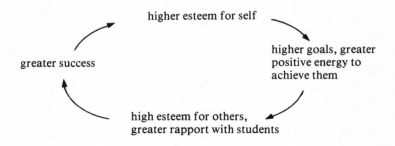

higher esteem for self

higher goals, greater positive energy to achieve them

greater success

high esteem for others, greater rapport with students

When a person lacks self-esteem, he can try in many ways to hide his negative view of himself. One individual will work for an advanced degree, another aims at winning a competition, and still anothers sews on "ego patches" with his compulsive working for honors and citations. The person who feels bored with himself, empty, or unworthy is usually restless. He overworks or compensates to escape from his real self. However, as a man builds esteem and love for himself, as he begins to see himself as a worthy, loving, and caring person, he establishes his integrity. He begins to develop a rich and powerful center to his personality.

There seems to be a great distance between the fourth and fifth levels in Maslow's ladder of needs. The fourth need, which can be felt early in life, can also be satisfied then. The fifth need is not totally met until later in life. This fifth need, the urge for freedom and self-fulfillment, arises when a person grapples with various facets of his personhood and experiences a need to break out of rigid conformity. He craves spontaneity, release, naturalness, self-acceptance, and openness to life.

In the midst of fragmenting forces that pull the music educator in many directions, the maturing individual who begins to establish his integrity feels the urge to become the unique person he was meant to be. He feels driven to become in actuality what he is potentially. He begins to balance his sense of self and his sense of others, between independence and interdependence. In a free, creative climate he can seek and find this balance in his life.

The highest needs of all people are the cognitive needs. Because music educators usually have high intelligence, their mind-needs are very keen. The urge to reason, to find structure—cause and effect, or basic underlying relationships—is likely to be a strongly felt need in people who dedicate themselves to the teaching of music.

> The less a man is able to discover a goal for his life, the more he speeds the pace of his living.[15]

BREAKDOWN OF RAPPORT:
MOCK SATISFACTION OF NEEDS

The needy person who is ashamed of having human needs finds it necessary to satisfy them by subtle, subconscious maneuvers. He relegates to his subconscious his real needs and feelings and creates a very strict censorship, preventing this material from becoming conscious to him. All people, to some extent, protect themselves from the full knowledge of their deep-seated selfishness and uneasiness. All human beings, then, to some degree, resort subconsciously to defensive ways of comforting themselves and easing the burdens of life.

Masks Teachers Wear

Some teachers, afraid to relate to themselves or others, hide behind facades or masks. The term *mask* refers here to a need-denial as well as to a role enactment which is in opposition to one's true inner state.

The Good Teacher Mask. Many teachers adopt the "professional competency" mask. They want to be considered as dedicated, excellent teachers and highly skilled music specialists. They think of themselves as efficient workers who really get things done. They feel the urgency of producing students who perform, read, and are knowledgeable in the study of music. Although such teachers usually have a ready smile for students, the pleasant exterior is useful to them mainly in manipulating students to cooperate in their programs.

When on the job, a "good teacher" considers himself an efficiency machine which generates musical skills and facts. His function consists of setting off musical behaviors in other machines, called students. Although no teacher would use these words, any educator who cares mainly for what students produce does not act humanly toward them. He does not care to be personally present to them.

A clue to the presence of this mask is the hostility a teacher shows

46

toward a nonproducing student. When a teacher condemns or rejects his slow or nonworking students in his casual conversations, he betrays his lack of personal involvement with students. The humane teacher, in contrast, may be angry and frustrated at a student's lack of progress; but he respects the right in every person, young or old, to make personal choices in life. He stands by the student as teacher and helper.

The Nice Person Mask. Music educators can be charming, enthusiastic, and stimulating people. They can be "nice" people who, through their flashy personalities, can get music out of almost anyone. A people pleaser, or social-personality type of teacher, usually captivates the attention of students in "fun" experiences and is very popular.

The educational results of such an approach, however, can be superficial. A teacher who tends to think of classes or lessons as fun experiences is probably considering only the here and now and not the future of the student. His procedures often lack sequence, structure, and depth. Because of his focus on pleasing others, such a teacher fears to take the risk of procedures which might fail and tear away his mask of "nice person."

Another bad effect of such teaching behavior is that the personal maturity of the teacher remains that of a child of about ten whose life is governed principally by outside influences.[16] Although the teacher may be oblivious to the fact that no significant education is occurring, students quickly sense the weakness of the "fun" teacher. They flatter; they "snow" the teacher with pleasant talk and gifts; they effectively avoid learning. Meanwhile, the teacher believes he is a nice person and his students are becoming nice like him.

The Authority Mask. People who are very lonely and do not satisfy their need for intimate friendship can readily hide behind an authoritarian mask. Relatively out of touch with their own humanness, such teachers believe and act as if they were supreme in both music and education. Morally perfect, musically sensitive, and pedagogically correct, the authoritarian teacher feels he is always right. However, students resent the hypocrisy of such people, and they experience little really significant learning when dealing with such teachers. Herbert Kohl writes, "The ideal of the teacher as a flawless . . . exemplar is a devilish trap for the teacher as well as a burden for the child."[17]

Games Teachers Play

When a person has unresolved conflicts or unmet needs and refuses to face these consciously, his subconscious goes to work. He engages in many games and self-feeding activities which diminish his ability to relate to himself and others genuinely. Individuals who provoke put-downs, enjoy flattery and attention, selfishly seek self-gratification and self-gains even at the expense of the student and "cop out" in subtle ways betray the fact that they are not meeting their needs for security and love in a truly adult way. Men and women the world over find themselves unable to relate to others in a mature way and regress to methods of obtaining every bit of mothering they can squeeze out of other people. Such people have little respect for themselves or others.

Eric Berne believed that no one is capable of game-free existence. However, he believed, too, that a person can substitute "good games" for underhanded ones. A crucial idea underlying this change is that the immature conduct is rewarded by pseudo acceptance and momentary excitement, which lighten one's burden. Until his more mature, self-enhancing behaviors are equally rewarding and more satisfying than his childish maneuvers, a person will not change.

> The tragedy for the most of us is that our defenses keep us from being aware of this rationality, so that consciously we are moving in one direction while organismically we are moving in another.[18]

Defense Mechanisms

When a person is not at peace inside, his behavior shows it. If he worries about his reputation as a music teacher or any other personal problem, he will probably engage in many psychological defenses to protect himself from having to face uncomfortable thoughts and feelings. Defense mechanisms are those subconscious, face-saving devices which people use to try to reduce conflict between their own inner state of ungratified needs and the necessity of having a facade of success and competence.[19]

For example, a teacher feels defensive and hurt when his students are criticized in competition. He may protect himself from that hurt with a variety of mechanisms. One teacher may rationalize his poor ratings by saying that the students needed the failure. Another man completely projects the blame on the judge or the circumstances. The next man may compensate for the loss by refusing to admit his weakness in teaching, and play up his other strengths. Another individual may use escapist techniques and refuse to discuss the issue. Still another may use the technique of introjection. He joins with the criticism (although he does not believe it) and turns against the student. What does the well-adjusted man do? Trying to strengthen his teaching, he admits his disappointment, reevaluates his techniques, and goes on with renewed effort and insight.

Although all teachers are sensitive and defensive at times, there are many who, for the most part, are well-adjusted. These individuals are able to admit their needs honestly to others and receive acceptance and security from interstaff relationships as well as from encounters with family, friends, and students. They are in touch with their own feelings as well as sensitively aware of how others feel. Knowing the situation enables them to use emotional powers to energize the musical and educative setting.

> If music-expression has a curative effect, it
> should heal the teacher first.

UTILIZATION OF NEGATIVE FEELINGS IN TEACHING

Inside each individual runs a constant flow of information which bears watching. As the day goes on, that stream of data may report: "I am frustrated," or "I am happily surprised." There are no two people who have the same flow of feelings, nor does any person ever have the same flow twice. These feelings are part of one's most intimate self. Because they indicate to an individual his unique personhood, every person must treasure his instinctive feelings and use them to care for himself. Just as his sleepiness drives him to bed, so his angry feelings may show him where his priorities lie.

Passion is the energizer of purpose.[20]

Befriending Feelings

Sometimes a person's turbulent feelings are so uncomfortable that he wants to escape by denying them. Losing contact with disturbing feelings, however, means that a person is out of touch with his pleasant feelings and valuable inner potential, too. He becomes a "cold brain" and a robotlike individual. Further, hiding these feelings from oneself brings on an alienation from reality which, in turn, may lead to physical and mental illness.

Can any person admit, without embarrassment, all of his feelings? Can he be proud to have even his negative and aggressive feelings? If he truly loves himself as a whole person, he gladly accepts all these feelings as indicators of who he is and what he aims and fights for.

Only by honestly facing his feelings can he adequately integrate them into the totality of his life. Feelings are friends. The person who truly loves himself is proud of his feelings, no matter how shameful, weak, or imperfect these feelings seem to be. Feelings cannot lie. There is a deep cause which stimulates a person to feel as he does. Sometimes an unmet need triggers off negative reactions. Find the feeling. Find the cause of a reaction. A devil named is a devil expelled. Finding the source of a disturbing feeling saves needless pain, fatigue, and conflict in personal and professional circles.

By valuing feelings and inner motivations, positive or negative, a person learns his unique attitudes and values. He begins to delight in making satisfying and consistent choices. Gradually, as he becomes integrated, he drops masks and facades and becomes honest and genuine with others. He begins to trust his feelings as valuable indicators of just who he is and how he should act. He is able to respond to teaching demands and establish relations with others and still remain an "all-in-one-piece" integrated person.

Channeling Anger

Anger, an emotional excitement induced by intense displeasure, can fragment a person and seriously shatter his efforts to teach or deal with people. Because an angry person feels a need to avenge or punish, his body produces a substance, adrenalin, which stimulates him and enables him to take revenge on the "enemy." Since he feels extra emotional excitement as well as strong adrenal stimulation, a person is more alive when he is angry.

An angry person is a powerful person. However, an angry teacher must have insight into his anger before he can channel his energies into his work.

Suppose Mrs. Vulcan, the private teacher, runs out to empty her garbage before her piano students start coming for lessons.

From her backyard a neighbor, Mrs. Furrow, calls to her and delays her by some irrelevant talk. The "friend" not only detains the teacher, but disturbs her with a few subtle insinuations about her style of living.

As Mrs. Vulcan enters her house she notices that she is experiencing an inner commotion and excitement. "Oh, I am so angry at you, Doris Furrow," she mutters half-aloud later as she unlocks the front door. "I feel like a little child getting a spanking when you criticize me in such underhanded ways." Then, as she gains insight into her reaction, she finds relief in a pseudo revenge by thinking, "Well, I'll show you I'm not a child. I'm going to be the most effective piano teacher you ever saw."

Mrs. Vulcan feels put together, integrated, now. As she experiences new courage in her desire to be an excellent teacher, the stimulating adrenalin in her body reinforces her physical and mental strength. Because of this extra energy she becomes more involved physically and emotionally during lessons. She feels emotional power within her and channels her vitality, stimulating others in positive ways.

If, however, Mrs. Vulcan had been annoyed by Mrs. Furrow's remarks and had not dealt with her emotional state, she would have become more susceptible to further irritations that day. Her anger could have built into fury if she had experienced a series of provoking incidents in close succession. If one student had forgotten her books, another had forgotten her lesson, and her husband had chosen not to come home, she could have become almost irrational in her angry outbursts. By repressing her anger she would have enkindled it. The buildup could be diagramed thus:

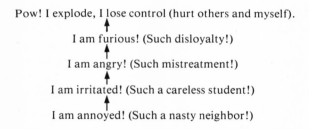

Pow! I explode, I lose control (hurt others and myself).

I am furious! (Such disloyalty!)

I am angry! (Such mistreatment!)

I am irritated! (Such a careless student!)

I am annoyed! (Such a nasty neighbor!)

Before he can control and channel anger, however, the educator must have an accepting attitude toward his feelings. He must accept the fact that students make him angry. He must always be proud of his feelings, even his angry feelings, because they are a part of himself, a concerned man whose life has meaning. Finally, the teacher must know that he is a free person who is entitled to live as a human being. He wants to be honest and real in dealing with students. Expressing angry feelings in a nonthreatening way, the teacher allows students to feel free and able to attack the work to be learned. He releases them from the distraction of having a teacher whose conduct is confusing and threatening.

> ... don't be afraid. Ain't nothing in the woods
> going to hurt you if you don't corner it or it don't
> smell that you are afraid.[21]

Channeling Anxiety

The harassed music teacher, worried and pressed for time, tends to fix his attention on the future. He feels a persistent dread of disasters or failures which could happen to him.[22]

In channeling such an anxiety, a teacher transforms his negative feelings into an energetic concern for the here-and-now performance. The wise teacher harnesses his emotional power and becomes more sensitive and aware of the present. In this way he improves both his present circumstances as well as his chances for future success.

Suppose Mr. Shift is standing on his podium waiting for the choir to settle down. He thinks about the contest next week. Will his choir get a "star" rating? Then he realizes that the "star" rating depends upon the tone, balance, and expressive qualities of his group. Why not check each of these qualities? He selects specific points and concentrates on these with full attention. By intensifying his positive efforts, he uses the energy stirred up by negative emotions and achieves both the joy and satisfaction of better performing and greater hope of success in the contest.

Anxiety causes severe problems in music studios and classrooms. Students sense the panicky feelings of the teacher and become nervous and aimless, and sometimes lose interest. They react more slowly; tend to sing or play sharp; and because of the bodily imbalance which nervousness brings, fail to keep a steady beat. Students learn less when their attention is divided between learning music and trying to figure out why the teacher is so anxious. When their music instructor is honest and genuine with them, students have the freedom to focus completely on their music.

Channeling Insecurity

By and large, most music educators like the "top dog" level of success. To obtain this, they take risks which make them feel insecure. Their insecurity, like any emotion, stirs up and stimulates these persons. This extra energy need not be wasted. Teachers can transform it into the motivating power which will spur students on to the success they, too, desire.

A piano teacher may slow a student down to a tempo realistic for him by saying, "John, I'd feel safer at this speed." A classroom music teacher may admit, "I really am not too sure I can make it through this song. You'll help me if you can, huh?" If remarks like these tend to relax both teacher and class, they are useful. Students respect teachers who are honest.

Some insecure persons are overcautious. Others are unrealistically ambitious. Some fear taking risks and frustrate students with monotonous, unchanging procedures. Others overestimate their ability and "ride" the students, pressing for higher achievements. Insecure teachers can either be tyrants or parasites. They can act like big bosses or like possessive owners of students. They can also be sycophants who in "mousy" ways coax supportive or flattering statements from students.

Teachers do well to examine in which ways insecurity is harming them and others. When they can face their feelings of fear and uncertainty, they can channel them into positive energy. By achieving little goals, a person attains assurance. Step by step, the insecure person acquires higher self-esteem and greater success in teaching.

> It is only with the heart that one sees rightly;
> what is essential is invisible to the eye.
>
> Saint-Exupéry

The Test of Maturity

Upon examining themselves, most persons find a great deal of childish behavior in their lives. The anger, jealousy, desire, stubborn streaks as well as the wonders of childlike thought and behavior continue to be relived in adult life. The parental taboos and sanctions also live on, demanding a certain amount of fixed behavior. With constant vigilance and sturdy effort, a maturing person brings these influences under the control of his adult reasoning. The adult is slowly freed from parental "hangups" and childish emotional instability. The adult carries with him a certain spontaneity in being able to act appropriately. If he is at a party, he can be creative, buoyant, and mischievous. When in class he can be a nurturing parent. When he assesses reality and makes decisions, he calculates, weighs the evidence at hand, and reasons clearheadedly. At all times there is an interplay between societal norms, emotional reactions, and adult reasoning. Choosing the appropriate behavior is the test of emotional maturity.

The mature teacher maintains an appropriate balance between his feeling, judging, and reasoning processes. He accepts in himself the feeling states of a child, he adjusts himself to the moral and environmental norms, and he has a controlling reasoning process that measures the advisability of his thought and behavior choices.

However, this balance is difficult to maintain. It requires a sensitivity to one's own inner wisdom as well as a clear perception of the people and the situation. Maturity and balance are fruits of struggles, risks, mistakes, insights, and consequent adjustments.

Maturity not only brings to light what a person truly is; it helps him succeed in understanding, respecting, and winning the respect of others. The mature person is ready and willing to reach out to students with dedication and love. He is a person of vision and courage who, though he has all the tendencies of other human beings, is able to scrutinize and develop potential in students.

All the world's a stage
And all the men and women merely players.
They have their exits and their entrances;
Each man in his time plays many parts.
Shakespeare

As a teacher interacts with students and other adults, he is involved in a two-fold drama; he is on a double stage, so to speak. Not only does he act on the stage of public action—swayed by others' opinions and expectations—but he also performs on a private, inner stage within him, where he rehearses, plans, and chooses his behavior.[23]

The psychiatrist Eric Berne referred to the inner compulsions, the interior programming every person feels in acting out this personal drama as a "psychological script." Berne believed that a person's script—his stance toward himself and his destiny—dictates the inner and outer moves he makes.

The idea of self and role in life begins at birth and slowly evolves while, in this twofold drama, persons act and react to situations. Most people are totally aware that they are driven to make choices by this inner programming, and they do not realize that their feeling of autonomy is nothing more than an illusion.[24] Because of their unconscious, but real, preoccupation with following their star and achieving their life-goal, however, such people lack awareness, creativity, honesty, and perception, which could be theirs if they wished to investigate their inner motivational drama.

Scripts do simplify one's life. One person sees himself as an underdog and consistently behaves defensively. Another feels that he is "top dog" and tyrannizes others. One is a patient sufferer, another is a self-styled genius, and still another feels that he is a good-for-nothing. Letting oneself be carried along by the scripting adopted in childhood easily allows society to pigeonhole him. It is common social behavior to classify individuals and put them into small boxes, expecting consistent behavior from them. This expectation of immature, nonthinking conformity further limits persons from breaking out of their shells and enjoying rationally chosen patterns of behavior. Examples from literature abound which demonstrate how persons narrow their visions of themselves and thus limit their choices of conduct.

It is of utmost importance, therefore, that any teacher who wishes to become mature knows his own scripting. Perhaps the search for the answers to questions such as Who am I? What am I doing here? What do others mean to me? will take a lifetime of searching. Such an investigation may well start by reading self-help books on scripting by authors like George Harris, Muriel James, Eric Berne, and Claude Steiner.

Maturity, self-fulfillment, and a well-adjusted life will never come to a teacher who hides from his real self. On the contrary, the teacher who is brave enough to explore his hang-ups, to measure the power which others have on him; and to evaluate the force of his own inner compulsions as well as his own personal values, hopes, and feelings can become ever more free to live a creative and autonomous life. This is the person who is ready to educate others for the rich life which a musician can lead.

Notes

1. Barry Stevens and Carl R. Rogers, *Person to Person* (New York: Simon & Schuster, Pocket Books, 1967), p. 1.

2. Carl R. Rogers, *Coming into Existence* (New York: Dell Publishing Co., 1967), p. 21.

3. Robert R. Carkhuff, *Belly to Belly Back to Back* ed. by Bernard G. Berenson (Amherst, Mass.: Human Resource Development Press, 1975), p. 11.

4. Carl R. Rogers, *On Becoming a Person* (Boston: Houghton Mifflin Co., 1961), p. 110.

5. Gerald F. Corey, *Teachers Can Make a Difference* (Columbus, Ohio: Charles E. Merrill Publishing Co., 1973), p. 56.

6. Maxwell Maltz, *The Magic Power of Self-Image Psychology* (Englewood Cliffs, N.J.: Prentice-Hall, 1964), p. 127.

7. Helen Gum Westlake, *Relationships: A Study in Human Behavior* (Lexington, Mass.: Ginn and Co., 1972), p. 23.

8. Eric Fromm, *The Revolution of Hope* (New York: Harper & Row, Publishers, 1971), p. 159.

9. Sidney M. Jourard, *The Transparent Self,* p. 5.

10. Charles H. Ball, "Thoughts on Music as Aesthetic Education," *Toward an Aesthetic Education* (Washington, D.C.: Music Educators National Conference, 1971), p. 59.

11. Trafford P. Maher, *Lest We Build on Sand* (St. Louis: Catholic Hospital Association, 1966), p. 101.

12. Helen Gum Westlake, *Relationships: A Study in Human Behavior,* p. 3.

13. Adapted from Frank Goble, *The Third Force* (New York: Simon & Schuster, Pocket Books, 1970), p. 52.

14. *Ibid.*

15. Viktor E. Frankl, *Psychotherapy and Existentialism* (New York: Simon & Schuster, 1967), p. 126.

16. Eric Berne, *What Do You Say After You Say Hello?* (New York: Bantam Books, 1972), p. 158.

17. Herbert Kohl, *36 Children* (New York: New American Library, Signet Books, 1967), p. 25.

18. Carl R. Rogers, a note on "The Nature of Man," *Journal of Counseling Psychology,* IV (March 1957), 202. Copyright 1957 by the American Psychological Association. Reprinted by permission.

19. Westlake, *Relationships: A Study in Human Behavior,* p. 74.

20. David Seabury, *The Art of Selfishness* (New York: Simon & Schuster, Cornerstone Library, 1964), p. 170. ·

21. William Faulkner, *The Bear* (New York: Random House, 1944).

22. Lawrence C. Kolb, *Modern Clinical Psychiatry* (Philadelphia: W. B. Saunders Co., 1973), p. 111.

23. Frederick S. Perls, *Gestalt Therapy Verbatim* (Moab, Utah: Real People Press, 1969), p. 50.

24. Muriel James and Dorothy Jongeward, *Born to Win* (Reading, Mass.: Addison-Wesley Publishing Co., 1971), p. 79.

3

Measuring the Elements and Skills of Rapport

The unexamined life is not worth living.

Socrates

When a music teacher knows his own feelings, values, and relational stance, he can succeed in establishing and maintaining good rapport with his students. When he also knows which elements of rapport he is using to establish relationships, he enjoys more success in his relating experiences.

Since the various elements of rapport are largely attitudinal and relatively intangible, a teacher seeking to relate effectively with students may have a need to use concrete measuring tools in assessing his rapport. To what degree is he genuine? How could he become more congruent? Can he listen to students and really empathize with them? Does he accept them warmly and respectfully? What kinds of interaction go into his teaching procedures? The tools given in this chapter offer specific evaluation of a teacher's actual rapport-ability.

MEASURING THE ELEMENTS OF RAPPORT

When a person feels and experiences another's emotions, hurts, and joys, he is empathizing. A teacher who empathizes with a student shows that he has insight into the student's emotional and cognitive frame of reference. Because he is truly in touch with the student in his natural tendencies, the teacher can predict with some validity how this young person will learn. He knows of hereditary and environmental factors which influence him and condition, to some degree, his unique reactions and responses. In the example of Carrie Perkins (see chapter 2), Judy is an empathetic friend who helps Carrie accept her feelings and stimulates her to grow as a person.

Testing the Presence of Empathy

How does a teacher carry on an empathic conversation with a student? How can he enter into the student's world? The following conversation taken from a private setting demonstrates empathy. Notice how the student's feelings are mirrored in the teacher.

S: Hey, teach, do I hafta study Bach?

T: It seems you don't like Bach.

S: The dumb music has no meaning.

T: You think Bach doesn't say what you want to say?

S: Yeah. I'd like something with a good beat that doesn't spread all over the place.

T: Yes, I know how angry I get when my fingers fumble!

S: Gets me all off beat!

T: You feel the beat and hate to lose it.

S: Oh, I don't think I even feel a beat—I'm just no good at the piano.

T: It must hurt a lot to say that.

S: Yeah, but I'm good at other things—sometimes I think I should quit.

T: You feel a bit trapped between keyboard problems and the desire to learn piano.

S: I wish there were some way . . .

T: Suppose we find something which seems more meaningful but is less demanding and less frustrating this next week.

S: I'll buy that—whatcha got?

The student's deeper problem—that of facing and accepting himself—emerges and dissolves because the teacher cares enough to listen and empathize.

The conversation could have proceeded like this:

S: Hey, teach, do I hafta study Bach?

T: Yes. I know you don't understand this, but the finger and tonal techniques demanded by Bach are necessary for your future study.

Here the teacher downgrades the experiences of the student and treats him as a thing. The nonempathic teacher does not care about the feelings of his student. Because of a lack of mutual understanding, this student cannot proceed with maximum efficiency. The lack of empathy in this teacher may have cost him one of his best students.

In ranking the levels at which teachers can empathize with students, Dr. David Aspy stratifies teacher responses into five levels. The following scale is an adaptation of his In-Service Scale made useful here for music educators.

EMPATHY SCALE*

Level 1 Teacher is dead wrong about estimation of feelings; no communication by word or tone of voice as to his own feelings (blank stare).

Teacher responds without feeling, merely giving orders, telling, criticizing in a flat, monotonous tone.

Level 2	Slight evidence of feelings shown by teacher. Estimation of student feeling somewhat correct; no mention of teacher's feeling.	Words try to convey the emotion expressed. "Hold it down," teacher says in a controlling voice. Effort to argue with his experience, lessen it, deny it.
Level 3	Teacher's *tone* of voice matches the feeling of students; he's "with it" but no word used to express teacher's feeling.	Teacher says, "Good" when students show excitement, joy. Teacher neither adds nor detracts.
Level 4	Tone of voice matches the feelings of students. Uses mild words to describe his own feelings.	Teacher adds slightly to meaning of students by appropriate words, "Good. You really enjoy performing."
Level 5	Tone of voice conveys feelings of student. Uses strong words to describe his own feelings.	Teacher adds much to meaning of student's experience. "Great. I felt as if Beethoven were right in the room."

* Adapted from David N. Aspy, *Toward a Technology for Humanizing Education* (Champaign, Illinois: Research Press Co., 1972), pp. 55-56.

Testing for Genuineness

When trying to specify behaviors as genuine, the analyst simply detects personal and honest words or actions as opposed to those of a mechanical, impersonal nature. A teacher who is noncommittal about personal feelings hides behind an authoritarian role for many reasons. Music teachers can crawl into a shell inside themselves when students are repulsive, uneducable or uncooperative. Afraid to speak honestly, they tend to act as teachers, not as human beings, when they have to deal with students from the following groups: students of the opposite sex; students who persist in tardiness or truancy; students who are unkempt; students who are

62

deceptive, tricky, or disloyal; or, finally, students who learn slowly or very little.

A teacher endeavoring to study genuineness in his behavior does well to examine his attitudes, prejudices, and limiting beliefs. In which ways is he closed, fixed, and rigid? Does he see the real persons who are his students or just their behavior? Does he admit that he may be narrow in his thinking? A teacher who is open and honest with students admits his prejudice as in the following example:

S: You don't like black people.

T: Come on now. I think I do. But what you're really saying is that I don't like *you*.

S: Right! Why, you don't even remember my name—you never forget the names of white students.

T: I'm sorry about that. But I really have trouble with names. Aren't you singling out things which prove your point?

S: You use high-sounding words about liking others, but you're really a fraud.

T: You mean I'm not perfect. But we're avoiding the issue of my feelings about you. You know, there are times when I don't like you because you embarrass others.

S: You're so smart. Why does that bother you?

T: Because I have feelings. I wonder if you know your feelings. It seems to me that you want me to dislike you— then you're safe in disliking me.

This teacher does not resolve the conflict, a problem which may defy solution. However, he is brave in his honest statement of just what the issue is. He does not hide behind the limiting belief that he must *like* all his students.

One of the most frustrating obstacles to genuine relationships is the feeling that teachers must like their students. They know their negative feelings about students and are plagued with the felt necessity of *liking* students in order to teach them. Such teachers experience an internal conflict between the real self and the ideal self within them. The real self cringes from associating with some

63

students. The ideal self "likes" all the students. This inner battle, heightened by a teacher's need to reach the student, leads to confusion for the student. He sees a teacher verbalizing messages of acceptance while showing dislike for him in subtle nonverbal signs. Students are more upset over this dichotomy than they would be over the truth, even the ugly truth. There is safety and some possibility of prediction in knowing the truth.

Scale of Analysis

In analyzing genuineness the analyst divides teaching behaviors into two classes: the role behavior and the personal behavior of a teacher. Although it is somewhat easy to detect phoniness in a person, it is more difficult to discern genuine authenticity in a teacher. In the following scale the behaviors begin in Level 1 with low-genuine or role behavior and extend to high-genuine behavior, which consists of spontaneous, personal encountering of students.

SCALE OF GENUINENESS IN A TEACHER*

Level 1	All communication is formal, ritualistic; seems mechanical.	Sounds like schoolteacher in tone, word choice, and manner: "Turn to page 5 and take it from K . . ."
Level 2	Most communication is ritualistic, but a few remarks are in a casual, normal tone of voice.	Some vitality and spontaneity in tone and word choice.
Level 3	Half and half: role and personal verbal behavior.	Neither enthusiastic nor dull.
Level 4	More spontaneous than ritualistic verbal behavior.	Rarely the schoolteacher's tone of voice; enthusiastic and inviting verbal behavior.
Level 5	All spontaneous communication; neither mechanical nor ritualistic.	Always engages in normal conversation; freedom-giving phrases.

* Adapted from Aspy, pp. 73-74.

Self-examination in this area can be embarrassing and painful for a teacher. Because he shrinks from the possibility of finding non-genuine behavior in his teaching, he may not evaluate himself objectively. Hence, it is quite necessary to meet with others to study genuineness. By observing a videotape or by inviting others to observe him while teaching, a teacher can obtain an objective and true appraisal.

> A child does not learn to love music from a teacher whom he hates. The teacher's emotional tone has a stronger echo than his musical instrument.[1]

Measuring Acceptance, Warmth, Respect

Most teachers are very eager to measure their accepting behaviors. Since they eagerly await students to join their groups and fear that their performers will drop out, they want to appear as accepting, attractive people.

However, are they accepting students or merely ensnaring them? Warmth, or acceptance, is a deep respect for the whole person. Warmth is a prizing reverence for a student because he has latent abilities and talents awaiting fulfillment. A teacher with respect places much emphasis on the involvement of the student in the class procedures.

In the analysis scale which follows, the quality of acceptance is measured by the criterion of respect for the student's ability to interact with learning. The accepting teacher stands back and, because he believes that the student can reach out and achieve learning and understanding, is effective in stimulating the process of learning.

For example, a class of Mexican teenagers met in my English song class. On this November day they were glum and unresponsive. I tried to stimulate remarks and statements of feelings, and these came:

"It is so dull and cold here in Minnesota."

"I can't be in the school play."

"The song is too high."

"It is hard to sing in English."

I showed my acceptance of them by asking their acceptance of me in return. "I really have a problem finding good songs in good keys today." They began to forget their negative feelings as they tried to help me find good English tunes and transpose them into comfortable ranges. They forgot their sadness and boredom when they found enjoyment in taking initiative in class. This mutual search proved to be a rewarding musical experience.

When a teacher accepts a student and respects his strengths as a person, he shows his value for the whole person. He believes that the student has high capacities for thinking, interpreting, and performing. He also believes the student needs meaningful tasks to develop these powers.

The following levels show the degrees to which one can demonstrate respect for the student's powers. One of the most powerful ways of growing in acceptance of others begins with the evaluation of that element. Only after one gains insight into his nonaccepting behavior patterns can he begin to act appropriately in relation to his evaluation.

SCALE OF ANALYSIS*

Level 1	Teacher has a negative regard for student capacity to learn.	"This is too difficult . . . I don't expect . . ." Class structured to stimulate little interaction.
Level 2	Somewhat negative regard for individual ability to operate effectively in learning situation involving lower-level skills of memory and recognition.	Teacher calls on others to help a pupil, does not expect a student to be able. "I'll decide for you; you listen and follow." Rote responses.

---

* Adapted from Aspy, pp. 88-89.

Level 3	Teacher shows positive regard for lower-level skills but not for higher-level intellectual processes of creativity, interpretation, judgment.	"You can play well, but I must decide on the interpretation."
Level 4	A consistent positive regard in deeming student able to respond on lower level tasks and occasionally expects higher level processes, too.	"You may even be able to think of . . ." Teacher expects student to contribute creatively.
Level 5	Teacher consistently communicates her respect for abilities of students toward tasks of all levels.	"Now, I *know* you can think of better ways to interpret this." Higher-level responses are encouraged and prized by the teacher.

The teacher of music often finds it necessary to dictate, lecture, and demonstrate. Although these teaching behaviors rank low in the scale of acceptance, they do not mean, necessarily, that the teacher is belittling a student's native ability. The scale has validity, however, because the teacher who constantly takes the initiative, talks most of the time, and makes all the decisions—the behaviors of Levels 1 and 2 of this scale—obviously minimizes the student's ability to interact with his learning.

This scale is usable in private as well as group analysis. Teachers can evaluate themselves or others by listening to tape recordings of their teaching sessions and rating their respect, or acceptance, objectively.

MEASURING THE SKILLS OF RAPPORT

The skills which enable a teacher to develop and maintain rapport are the practical techniques of listening and analyses of nonverbal and verbal interaction. By measuring the extent of his use of these techniques in relating to students, a teacher can further assess his degree of rapport.

> Listening is the key to the entrance to another's life; intensity is the key to listening.

Evaluation of Listening

Since listening to a student's verbal and nonverbal behavior is an essential technique in gaining information before relating to a student, a teacher may want to know how well he listens. By measuring his own ability to listen through an evaluation tool, he not only realizes his need for improvement, but sees specific behaviors which can heighten his perception.

Listening is the skill which enables one to feel empathy. By being able to notice by a student's inferences or by the nonverbal behavior what he seems to be feeling, a teacher is able to empathize with him. By being alert and perceptive to a student's thought, a teacher can develop a bond of rapport with him. The levels of a person's listening range from indifference toward the student's ideas and feelings to keen sensitivity and accurate perception.

THE LEVELS OF LISTENING*

How do I respond to feelings?	How do I catch his ideas?
1. I am totally unaware of his feelings.	1. I was dead wrong—completely missed.
2. I think I know.	2. I missed, just a bit.
3. I know his feelings adequately.	3. I get an accurate message.
4. I know his feelings better than he does.	4. I get the idea a bit more concisely than he.
5. I see deeper into student feelings than he and can provide him with a new view.	5. I see beyond the stated meaning—I know his insight.

*Norman A. Sprinthall, speech in Little Falls, Minnesota, August, 1973.

68

Teachers can implement the scale by watching a typical classroom scene on a videotape machine. Interested teachers focus their attention on only one student in the film and try to assess his ideas as well as his inner feelings and attitudes. The teachers share their impressions of this student and tell what they think he is feeling and saying. Then they assess how much of this the teacher in the film seems to be able to hear. They may replay the videotape to check the validity of their evaluation. Such discussion will clarify in a teacher's mind his level of listening as well as the specific ways in which he can improve.

Analyzing Nonverbal Behavior

How do teachers and students interact? First of all, teachers have a mysterious effect on students. Their bearing, manner of speech, choices of materials, procedures, and fixed standards create an atmosphere which either frees or inhibits the student. The teacher's nonverbal behavior signifies his relational stance and causes a definite subconscious reaction in the student. Often when a student cooperates, rebels, conforms, or shows his feelings by a variety of subtle nonverbal signs, he is reacting to a teacher's body language.

How can a teacher examine his body language? There are no evaluative tools in this recently stressed area. However, the following questions may provide some insights into the area of a teacher's sending messages through nonverbal communication.

1. How much space do I need around me? How do I show my sensitivity when people come "too near" me?
2. Do I violate the student's "inner space" by coming too near him and touching him when his nonverbal cues tell me to move away? Does he then think I am treating him as a non-person?
3. Do I jam students so close to each other that the only way they can tolerate this abuse of personal space is to consider themselves as non-persons?
4. Do I have defense mechanisms of escape? Do I look away from the scene so others think I did not see? Do I become quiet, sort of play dead?

5. Do I respect cues from students who rock in their chairs, swing legs, tap with fingers to let me know I am physically too close?

6. Do I invade the students' critical space, intending to do some harm? If so, I must expect them to strike back at me.[2]

7. Do I use color as a sign or a signal of my feelings? Color is a language governed by the subconscious. It goes from the teacher's subconscious to the student's subconscious without necessarily reaching the conscious level in anyone. A human procedure of dressing colorfully can improve the environment and resolve or quell academic problems.[3]

8. What about my face? Does it show my personal problems? What gestures do I commonly make? What do they seem to say? Do I wink? Why?

9. How do I usually walk? So fast that I look as if I never want to be where I am? So slow that I appear aimless and without goal? So jerkily that I appear anxious and worried?

10. What do my hands say? Do I snap my fingers or gesticulate nervously? Are my hands clumsy from nervousness and fear? Do I touch students who don't want to be touched?

11. Do I use my eyes to warm and encourage people or to hurt them? Do I realize that my eyes can give many messages? What do they seem to say and when?

12. Do I overdo gestures, such as shaking hands so enthusiastically that I raise the student's suspicion that I am not genuine?[4]

13. Do I give messages of boredom, disgust, and nonacceptance?

14. What is the emotional tone of my voice? Is it sarcastic? Does it build defenses or resentment in students? Do I make vulgar, fearful noises when I am angry?

15. Do I label students internally ("Jane can't learn.") and betray my negative attitudes with my body language?

A teacher who is determined to succeed in his job of educating does well to watch student reaction to his body language. Because much of what the body communicates is subconscious, a teacher does not know what his nonverbal behavior is saying. He cannot see his own image just as no man can see his own face except in a mirror. The teacher must look to student reaction for the truth of his own messages. Since the major part of setting the climate for learning and allowing the student the freedom to learn depends upon the teacher's nonverbal behavior and his listening habits, these techniques are extremely important for success in music education.

A thought which is at once stimulating and frightening is that students notice the whole person of the teacher. They do not listen much to what words he says. They watch nonverbal behavior and draw inferences because they are looking for the real man or woman who lives within that person. They want to see the anger, the passion and ecstasy of a teacher's personal life. They want to know the thoroughly human person speaking consistently and naturally to them through words as well as through body language. If they find such a teacher—one who is truly alive as a person—there is hope for new meanings and worthwhile changes in their lives.

> When a facilitator creates, even to a modest
> degree, a classroom climate characterized by all
> that he can achieve of realness, prizing and em-
> pathy; when he trusts the constructive tendency
> of the individual and the group, then he discovers
> that he has inaugurated an educational
> revolution.[5]

ANALYSIS OF ORAL INTERACTION

Because people relate, to a great extent, on the subconscious level, their relations are, in themselves, quite unmeasurable.

However, verbal behavior can signify not only the subconscious relational stance, but also the conscious objectives of a teacher. By studying the words which he and his students exchange, a teacher can learn his level of humanness. He is then in a position to remedy his weaknesses.

Interaction Analysis

The system of evaluation devised by Ned A. Flanders isolates ten typical kinds of verbal interaction. These categories of behavior do not usually overlap. Determining which types of interaction a teacher uses in his teaching encounters makes possible specific measurement.

Flanders divides educational behaviors into two broad categories: indirect and direct. When a teacher deals indirectly with students, he refrains from "show and tell" procedures; rather, he considers himself a facilitator or catalyst who speeds up and induces learning. He considers the learner to be a self-reliant human being who can reach out and grasp facts, skills, and insights with a minimum of help from the teacher. The direct teacher, on the contrary, demonstrates, lectures, and criticizes. He has fixed responses to his questions and expects conformity with his demands. Most teachers find both these types of interaction in their teaching behavior. Teachers in good rapport with their students tend to be indirect. However, they find it necessary to use direct interaction at times in order to be clear, brief, and efficient.

THE FLANDERS SCALE OF INTERACTION ANALYSIS*

Indirect Behaviors

1. Teacher accepts student's feelings.   ("You like it, huh?")
2. Teacher praises student.   ("Good work!")

---

* Adapted from N. A. Flanders, *Interaction Analysis in the Classroom—A Manual for Observers* (Michigan: University of Michigan, 1965), p. 7.

3. Teacher accepts or uses   ("Let's try your idea.")
   student ideas.
4. Teacher asks questions.

Direct Behaviors

5. Teacher lectures.   ("A tie is a . . .")
6. Teacher gives direction.   ("Don't play the second note!")
7. Teacher criticizes.   ("Careless! Watch the ties!")

Direct

8. Student responds as predicted. ("A tie is a . . .")
9. Student questions or responds
   creatively.   ("Why a tie?")

Miscellaneous

10. Silence or confusion.

By using Flanders Interaction Analysis, a teacher can easily determine the type of verbal interaction he uses when teaching. To do this he can make a tape recording of his teaching a class or private lesson. Later, when alone, with other teachers, or with his family, he can listen to his words and determine which behaviors dominated his teaching. He simply analyzes the message of a verbal statement and tabulates and lists the number of that behavior as listed in the scale. Another way of determining which behaviors a teacher is using is to ask an alert person to come into the class and observe and tabulate the types of interaction.

Here is an example of typical interaction taken from the beginning of a piano lesson:

Dialogue	Category of Behavior	Type of Behavior
T: My, Joe, you look sharp in that new outfit!	2	I*
S: Yeah, I gotta cheer myself up—lost the game last night!	9	I

T:	Disappointing, I know. But you played well.	1	I
S:	I'm so mad at those guys I could sock 'em in the jaw right now!	9	I
T:	Could we channel that anger into some powerful piece to warm up with?	4	I
S:	Great! How about the Chopin Polonaise?	9	I
	(Joe plays . . .)	8	D**
T:	Stop, Joe, I don't agree with that fingering.	7	D
S:	But I need it that way . . . see?	9	I
T:	I'll accept that *if* you . . .	3	I
S:	By the way, should I speed up that trill?	9	I
T:	Yes, try to do it like this . . .	5	D
S:	Like this?	8	D
T:	Excellent! Now put it into the piece.	2,6	I,D

	Total Indirect:	10	
	Total Direct:	5	Ratio: 2:1

The ratio here is 2 to 1 in favor of indirect behavior. The teacher is respectful in dealing with the student. He listens humanly to the student and allows him to learn in a self-directed way. However, he resorts to direct procedures when he feels it necessary or advisable.

Here is a contrasting example of interaction. The scene is a band rehearsal.

T:	Attention! Let's play the *Over-ture* first.	6	D
S:	Not again! We played it yester-day!	9	I
T:	You're not running my class! Get ready.	7,5	D,D
S:	(Students perform.)	8	D

---

* I = Indirect
** D = Direct

T: Cut! Clarinets, keep together.		
Don't rush!	6,7	D,D
S: (Performance improves.)	8	D
T: Much better. Now go back to		
letter K.	3,6	I,D
Total Indirect:	2	
Total Direct:	8	Ratio: 1:4

Chances are that this teacher will interact four times as often in a direct teaching behavior than an indirect one. However, this could just be a bad day when the teacher is pressed for time, anxious, angry about something, or working in a fatigued state.

Although band rehearsals usually require more direct interaction than private lessons, all music education settings demand a balance between the two kinds of behavior. Many private teachers are very direct; many band directors treat their students courteously and deal with them with respect.

Music in itself is a skill, an art, and a discipline. The very nature of the subject demands direct interaction behavior. However, if this is not balanced with accepting, warm, genuine behavior on the part of the teacher, the educative process becomes mechanical and meaningless.

Using Analysis as a Tool

Of the many uses analysis can have, its greatest use is as an in-service device which upgrades the efficiency and quality of teaching. If a teacher finds the experience of taping his teaching a bit uncomfortable, he can simply evaluate himself. He asks himself: In what instances did I accept student feelings and show this in my words? When did I praise my students today? Do my students feel free to ask creative questions and give spontaneous suggestions.

The tool is also very helpful for student teachers who wish to develop their ability to relate. College students who have no classes to work with may choose to stimulate interaction by role playing. Suppose Alice is trying to sell Barb a pencil while Carey watches. The following represents part of a possible three-minute period of interaction:

A:	I have a beautiful yellow pencil for you to buy.	5	D
B:	Yeah, I see . . .	8	D
A:	Hey, Barb, look, the color just matches that lovely yellow sweater you're wearing!	2	I
B:	Yeah, guess it does.	8	D
A:	You really like yellow?	4	I
B:	Goes with my hair.	8	D
A:	Wouldn't you like several pencils?	4	I

Total Indirect: 3
Total Direct: 4   Ratio: 3:4

Although such interaction does not have much personal significance, it gives these persons some insight into the relational impact of their words and questions. Perhaps further study of the categories would bring a clearer idea of their meaning and usefulness.

Clarification of Categories

The ten categories embrace both the indirect methods of stimulating a student to discover and retain learning as well as the direct methods of giving the students the facts or the verdicts of a teacher's judgment.

The first and third categories credit a teacher for his practice of listening and empathy. In the first he clarifies, predicts, or recalls student feelings, positive or negative, assuring the student that he is known, accepted, and respected. He frees the student to respond creatively; and when the student presents an original idea, as in category nine, the accepting teacher then scores in category three. At other times a teacher scores in this category when he facilitates student thinking by elaborating, clarifying, or building on student ideas, or by using student phraseology and slang. In these ways a teacher is working within the student's frame of reference, within his cognitive field.

Praising a student and his work by encouraging, reinforcing, and stimulating words is the behavior of category two. Somewhat related to this is the interaction described in category four, when a teacher asks questions, trusting that a student can answer. When a teacher asks questions, the students learn by discovering, recalling, or restructuring that which is to be learned in their own words or performance. In music settings there are creative ways of asking questions. A teacher can have students explore and experiment for sounds they want. At other times students discover new fingerings, analogies, creative analyses, or interpretations because of expert but subtle questioning by a teacher.

Direct interaction includes lecturing; giving of directions or guidance; and criticizing, or self-justifying. When an educator tells his student or class some facts, ideas, traditions, or trends, he expresses his own learning and views. Lecturing also includes the asking of rhetorical questions or the explaining of performing practices. Category six includes the giving of directions. This kind of behavior also includes teaching commands and guidance directions which are to be followed by immediate compliance, such as "Attention!" "Crescendo!" "Second ending!" or "Cut!" Finally, in category seven, a teacher criticizes or justifies himself. His statements tell students that their performance or ideas are not acceptable. Critical remarks may be judgmental, not only of a student's playing or singing; they may also be discourteous remarks about a student's personal behavior, his attitudes, his lack of respect, or his defiance.

In the last three categories the Interaction Analysis tool lists student behaviors which respond to the kind of interaction the teacher used. If the students feel freed by the indirect action of the teacher to respond enthusiastically and creatively, the analyst marks their response in category nine.

Clear-cut and predictable responses to teachers are those listed in category eight. In the last category, tuning, silence, or confusion may appear. An observer is unable to classify such behavior.

Significance of the Tool

Because the ten interacting behaviors of the Interaction Analysis system are so fundamental, so easy to observe, and not overlapping, the tool can be an effective source of information concerning teaching practices. By using this method a teacher can discover how he interacts with his students. He is then free to find reasons for his conduct. The ratio of his indirect-direct interaction can be indicative of his philosophy of teaching as well as of his concept of himself and his students.

If the teacher prizes the student as a self-directing and enterprising person and sees himself as a helper, facilitator, and mediator between the student and his learning, he is apt to score high in indirect behavior. If he thinks that his own learning is not infallible, but that many musical "facts" are evolving and ever in process, he will work indirectly with students, stimulating them to probe for new perspectives and insights.

On the contrary, the direct teacher thinks of himself as a trainer, fact-giver, disciplinarian, and authority. He believes students learn faster by being told and commanded. Because of this, he refuses to teach them as thinking and feeling human beings. They are performers, singers, and learners.

These extremes of philosophy—that of the facilitating teacher and that of the authoritarian teacher—do not exist in reality. Most teachers favor one or the other, but in practice shift pragmatically from direct to indirect behavior as the situation seems to require. At times it is urgent that a teacher be direct in his relating. However, if there is little indirect relating in a teaching situation, students often feel the learning is irrelevant because the atmosphere is impersonal.

Although the Interaction Analysis tool offers much data for personal and pedagogical introspection, it has one main weakness. It measures only verbal interaction. As indicated earlier, experts in the field of body language believe that people do not communicate primarily with words. However, at present there is no tool which adequately measures both kinds of behavior.

Interaction and Genuineness

How do the elements of personal honesty and teaching interaction correlate? Researchers have taken scores from Flanders Interaction Analysis tests and compared them to the results of the same teachers' scores on the Genuineness Scale. They found that there is a positive correlation between low-genuine people and directness in teaching approach. Those who rate as high-genuine, on the contrary, tend to praise more and stimulate student talk more than other teachers.[6] Although these tests were not administered to music teachers, there is good reason to believe that the interaction would be similar in music education settings.

Feedback from Students

A most useful tool of measurement is the student questionnaire. Students feel that they know their teachers, their warm acceptance and their respect as well as the nonpersonal behavior. Although their evaluations are at times biased and invalid, students' opinions and observations are usually helpful to a teacher in measuring rapport. In the preparation of a questionnaire for personal assessment, the following questions can be helpful to a teacher.

Empathy

1. Do you feel that I really notice your feelings?
2. Does it look as if I care how you are feeling?
3. Do you feel blamed when you show or express feelings?
4. Do I channel your feelings into proper outlets?
5. Do you sense that I am experiencing your feeling?
6. Do you think I express my feelings well?
7. Do I see your slant and point of view as well as my own?

Genuineness

1. Do I confuse you by saying things I don't seem to mean?
2. Do I seem so preoccupied with my own internal pressures that I am not free to respond to you?

3. Do I seem to be an honest person who admits feelings and personal limitations?
4. Do you feel like a person when I speak to you or do you feel as if something has to be done and you are the means of doing it?
5. Can you trust me and believe that I am honest?
6. Do I tell you my feelings honestly even if they tell of my disapproval of your behavior?

Acceptance

1. Do you think I believe in your ability to perform?
2. Do I accept your ability to choose original ways of doing things?
3. Do I respect your right to choose your own behavior provided that you learn and grow?
4. Do I "snap out" answers or directions rather than respect you as an intelligent student who can discover some things for himself?
5. Do I give you the liberty of being a human being in a climate of warmth and acceptance?
6. Do you feel I care for you for your own sake and not mine?

Measuring Interest in Rapport

A teacher betrays his attitude toward relating both in his professional and his private life. By listening to casual remarks said in an offhand manner, a sensitive teacher can detect interest or scorn for rapport. Any perceptive person, keenly aware of the advantages of good relating, can sense the subtle meaning of statements concerning the tolerance and guidance of young people. The following list of such statements includes statements heard at workshops and clinics. Some are good. Some show bad relating practices. As you read them, put a + before those which show some insight into good relating with students.

1. My kids play well: we only attempt what we can do.
2. I guess I spoil my kids. They wait for me to tell them answers and show them what to do.
3. My kids know my standards. They feel secure because they know what to expect.
4. My time is too precious to answer their constant "whys."
5. I tend to overlook a mistake or two with moderately talented students.
6. I find myself talking a lot while teaching.
7. When I strongly disagree with students, I feel I have to tell them.
8. It doesn't matter how kids feel: you have to *make* them do what is good for them.
9. I encourage parents to visit my lessons and classes.
10. I encourage my students to aim high. I think every child should aim at playing a concerto someday.
11. I learn almost as much from my students as they learn from me!
12. I hate contests and auditions because they put a great strain on me.
13. I need to buy much material because I like to give students a lot of choice in what they want to play and sing.
14. A teacher is a mastermind. Get others to think like you do and teaching is a snap.
15. I love to mix with my kids at parties as well as in teaching situations.
16. I wonder why students tremble at their lessons.
17. I find it hard to teach a student until I really know him.
18. I *make* my kids practice. If they don't, I "get after" the parents.
19. I haven't had a very good background for teaching but I accept myself.
20. My kids like me. They seem to absorb my ideas, attitudes; and it's fun to work with them because they are so like me.
21. Students, especially teenagers, get along with me because they know I accept and respect them.

22. I help students a lot; and they cling to me, expecting a lot, it seems.
23. My kids are free. If they feel an interpretation, I let them keep it—within limits, of course.
24. Why are kids so lazy these days?
25. I am so happy when my kids find personal expression in their music, I can overlook their mistakes.
26. The music class is no place for humorous or jovial talk.
27. Choosing and buying materials is a big job. I just can't feel comfortable giving last year's music this year.
28. I use the Smith method for everybody. It is easier to classify students if you use the same materials with all students.
29. I'm glad my kids do well in contests, but I am more glad that they find music meaningful.
30. I know my stuff. If the kids don't learn, that's their fault.

Did you have plus signs before number 1, 3, 5, and all the other odd-numbered statements? Did you detect the subtle references to rapport in these items? Did you sense a lack of respect and acceptance for students in the even-numbered statements and questions?

> The sterility and joylessness of so many schools
> in our country cannot but depress the children
> and adults who spend their time there.[7]

EVALUATION OF RAPPORT ITSELF

Does rapport really make a significant difference in improving music education? Does it heighten student's ambitions and hasten their progress in learning music?

Do Students Learn More in Rapport Situations?

Experience proves that those students who excel in music study are those who experience good rapport with their teachers. In the warmth of a loving and accepting teacher, these students eagerly reach out for higher skills and understanding. Is it because they relate well to the teacher or because they are talented? There are many talented people who do not succeed in music study; therefore, it may be safe to conclude that those who thrive do so because they find relationships stimulating and programs relevant.

Researchers, too, have tested the value of rapport. Studies show a positive correlation between the cognitive growth of students and levels of teacher-offered empathy.[8] Other studies demonstrate that high-genuine behavior in a teacher is related to an enhancement of self-image and academic achievement.[9,10,11] One such study[12] discovered an inverse correlation between bad relating experiences and success. Aspy writes:

> The data indicates that a teacher who provides high levels of facilitative conditions tends to enhance students' cognitive growth, but a teacher who provides low levels of these conditions may retard students' learning. That is, they tend to learn *less* than they normally would when they receive low levels of facilitative interpersonal conditions from their classroom teachers.[13]

Further tests[14] show a positive correlation between indirect teaching and achievement, higher verbal creativity, higher levels of critical thinking and the development of scientific attitudes in students.

> The findings indicated that students' use of their higher cognitive processes (problem-solving, etc.) is significantly and positively related to the teacher's levels of interpersonal conditions. This relationship is particularly strong in regard to positive regard. Apparently, since thinking aloud is a kind of interpersonal risk, a person tends to do this more frequently when he is sure he is valued.[15]

Since truancy and drop-out rate is a sensitive area for music educators,[16] the following study may cite some causes of this problem. This study reveals the correlation between school absences and good rapport:

> A second aspect . . . explored the relationship between the teachers' facilitative levels (Empathy, Congruence, Positive regard) and their students' daily absence. The findings revealed an inverse and

significant relationship between these variables. This led us to think that there may be some relationship between "school phobia" and the interpersonal skills of the teacher.[17]

Another factor which eases music teaching and allows students to learn more in conditions of good rapport is prediction. Teaching becomes simple and less threatening when an instructor begins to know the inner workings of students and attains the ability to predict their behavior. When students become transparent and understood by their teachers, their behavior is much more predictable. By being in touch with a student's inner motivational power and direction, the teacher can estimate the amount and quality of future performance and make realistic plans. Because such teachers can deal with known commodities, they do not feel the threat of the unknown and possibly disastrous future failures.

Attaining the Skills to Create Rapport?

First of all, chances are that if the reader is already a somewhat successful teacher, he has the qualities which Klausmeier lists for good teachers:

> Interest in verbal activities and fine arts, . . . a warm personality, good emotional adjustment and enthusiasm for teaching have been reported as characteristics of the more effective teachers.[18]

Klausmeier goes on to report that although teacher preparation programs scrutinize a student teacher's intellectual ability, total grade-point average, subject matter preparation, etc., research proves that these qualities correlate negatively with success in teaching: "Many teachers who have a low degree of these qualities rate higher than others in teacher success."[19] Chances are that these latter teachers are more personally present to their students and relate more humanly to them.

Yet a person who is gifted intellectually can very effectively attain the skill of creating rapport. David Aspy, who has trained many teachers in the skill of relating, finds it almost impossible to detect whether a person relates well naturally or because of

84

training. Relating, he says, is like cooking—simply follow the directions.[20]

However, the sequence of steps in attaining rapport is not

idea ⟶ behavior ⟶ habit ⟶ success.

Rather, a teacher must learn experientially that rapport pays off. First, he notices nonverbal behavior or the verbal inferences of his students, and then he steers the flow of the class to suit student goals and expectations. When he finds that relating to students really brings success, he says to himself, "Aha! It works!" This whets his appetite for more such rewarding behavior. The sequence, in reality, is usually thus:

successful action ⟶ attitude ⟶ habit ⟶ more success.

Teachers can count on success, too, because they are, as a whole, very tenacious in pursuing their goals. Once they realize that, their students enjoy them more and achieve more in classes and lessons; once they gain the insight that students do not want them to be perfect, and are prepared to live with their shortcomings, they can relax and be themselves. As Edward Ladd writes:

> Teachers more than anyone else have the capabilities and, deep down, the human understanding needed to develop better ways of treating kids; if they can establish the right kind of relationship, kids will put up with a lot of nonsense.[21]

How, Exactly, Does a Teacher Begin?

A specific task which is easy to measure and rather simple to incorporate into one's teaching is looking into the eyes of students. Although it seems to be a natural habit, Aspy found in his studies that only twenty percent of teachers measured could maintain eye contact with anyone for more than a fleeting second. Most teachers completely avoided looking into the eyes of students. Since most teachers do not use this valuable tool for meeting students, many a teacher could set a specific goal such as: I will establish eye contact at least half of the time within my first year of effort.

The other skills of listening and noting vocal inflections, inferences of words and meanings or nonverbal behavior can be made specific. A teacher who wants to relate tries to make himself more approachable by not cutting students off or by trying to empathize with their feelings. He can make it a specific goal to take time with students, to learn where they are "at" and make specific plans for where they want to go.

One handy place to begin is with one's failure. Why are students not trying to learn? It is easy to blame the home, environment, or other teachers. However, some students succeed even in the most unfortunate situations. A teacher can become angry; he can blame and scold the student. On the other hand, he can examine himself and check the availability of purposeful activity for this particular student. Is he communicating enough with this boy or girl to know how to teach him? If the teacher looks over his roll and picks out his five most "lazy" students and begins to relate to them, he will probably improve his skills. A specific goal for such a teacher is to challenge himself to the task of encountering and relating well with all students whom he is tempted to call "lazy." His goal consists of meeting those people and energizing them.

Failure is a good teacher. Every dropout proves that teachers do not succeed. One specific plan to correct this situation would be for the teacher to call each dropout into a private interview and try to relate to them. Invariably teachers find deep relational causes for student apathy and terminations. For many teachers this means less money in their pockets.

As the teacher slowly attains the skills of rapport, he becomes a better teacher as well as a more fully functioning person. Studies prove that teachers who have empathy, genuineness, and acceptance also rank high on tests such as Jourard's self-disclosure tests.[22]

> There is a kind of convergence of data which is mutually supportive and all of it points to the conclusion that the highest forms of human behavior are interrelated. For example, when the audio tapes were evaluated for teacher self-disclosure as formulated by Jourard, these results correlated positively and significantly with the teachers' levels of interpersonal functioning.[23]

The teacher striving for rapport is always learning about himself and how others react to him; he is constantly seeking more successful patterns of behavior. He realizes that when a student performs well, he is rewarded, but he does not waste time in self-congratulation. One success gives him the drive to move on to more successes.[24]

Although much of the research on rapport is as yet unpublished, there is sufficient evidence in such studies that a good relationship between teacher and student is an effective determinant in good education.[25,26]

Notes

1. Haim G. Ginott, *Between Parent and Child,* p. 96.

2. James J. Thompson, *Beyond Words,* p. 32.

3. James J. Thompson, "Color in the Classroom," *Beyond Words,* pp. 58-83.

4. Harold D. Lyon, Jr., *Learning to Feel—Feeling to Learn* (Columbus, Ohio: Charles E. Merrill Publishing Co., 1971), p. 80.

5. Carl R. Rogers, *Freedom to Learn* (Columbus, Ohio: Charles E. Merrill Publishing Co., 1969), p. 115.

6. David N. Aspy, *Toward a Technology for Humanizing Education,* p. 79.

7. Bennett Reimer, "Putting Aesthetic Education to Work," *Music Educators Journal* 59 (September 1972), 30.

8. *Ibid.,* p. 64.

9. E. V. Powell, "Teacher Behavior and Pupil Achievement," *Classroom Interaction Newsletter* (May 1968), 34.

10. W. A. Weber, "Teacher Behavior and Pupil Creativity," *Classroom Interaction Newsletter* (May 1968), 34.

11. J. B. Campbell, "Cognitive and Affective Process Development and Its Relation to a Teacher's Interaction Ratio" (unpublished doctoral thesis, New York University, 1968).

12. David N. Aspy, "The Effect of Teacher-Offered Conditions of Empathy, Congruence, and Positive Regard upon Student Achievement," *Florida Journal of Educational Research* XI (1969), 39-48.

13. _____ and Flora N. Roebuck, "From Humane Ideas to Human Technology and Back Again Many Times," *Education* 95 (November-December 1974), 165.

14. _____, "An Investigation of the Relationship Between Levels of Cognitive Functioning and the Teacher's Classroom Behavior," *Journal of Educational Research* 54 (May 1972).

15. _____ and Flora N. Roebuck, "From Humane Ideas to Human Technology and Back Again Many Times," p. 167.

16. _____ and W. Hadlock, "The Effect of High and Low Functioning Teachers upon Students' Performance," *Beyond Counseling and Therapy* by R. R. Carkhuff and B. Berenson (New York: Holt, Rinehart and Winston, 1967).

17. _____ and Flora N. Roebuck, "From Humane Ideas to Human Technology and Back Again Many Times," p. 165.

18. Herbert Klausmeier and Richard E. Ripple, *Learning and Human Abilities* (New York: Harper & Row, Publishers, 1971), p. 252.

19. *Ibid.,* p. 245.

20. David N. Aspy, "The Humane Implications of a Humane Technology" (Paper read at the ASCD convention March 18, 1975, New Orleans, Louisiana.)

21. Edward T. Ladd, "Teachers as Cause and Cure of Student Unrest," *Controversies in Education* (Philadelphia: W. B. Saunders Co., 1974), p. 470.

22. Sidney M. Jourard, *Self-Disclosure: An Experimental Analysis of the Transparent Self* (New York: Wily-Interscience, 1971), pp. 189-191.

23. David N. Aspy and Flora N. Roebuck, "From Humane Ideas to Human Technology and Back Again Many Times," pp. 163-171.

24. G. M. Della Piana and N. L. Gage, "Pupils' Values and Validity of the MTAL," *Journal of Educational Psychology* XXXVI (1955), 167-178.

25. R. M. Traverse, *Essentials of Learning* (New York: Macmillan Co., 1963).

26. D. Prescott, *The Child in the Educative Process* (New York: McGraw-Hill, 1957).

4

Meeting the Needs
of Students

Music is little more than the projection of the
ideas and emotions of a human being. The
responsibility of the teacher to enter into the
humanness of the student is, therefore, extremely
important.

Many teachers believe that it is wise to remain distant and aloof
from the person of the student. After they test IQ or talent by standard procedures, they feel they "know" the student and can
adequately select teaching procedures for him. The growing unrest
in music programs, however, may indicate that students taught in
an impersonal atmosphere find music study quite irrelevant and
meaningless.

Stop, Look, and Listen

Three points to remember in getting to know student needs are
these:
1. *Stop* being artificial in expecting a student to fit your norms.
Stop being judgmental and authoritarian. Stop boasting about
yourself and what you, the teacher, can do and have done for
others. Stop wearing the invisible sign: "I Am the Teacher." Stop
merely teaching literature and focusing on its consumption.

2. *Look* at the student's nonverbal behavior. His whole body is speaking. With his body the student is revealing his need for safety, security, and fulfillment. Look at his eyes, his gestures, and his facial expression. See the boredom, the nervousness, or the eager longing for acceptance and respect. See the needs, the aims, and the goals of the student.

3. *Listen* to the student. Interview him by gently stimulating him to speak of his concerns, goals, and learning patterns. Listen to him and show by your calm, kind manner that he is free to be himself in your music lessons or classes.

Naturalness Generates Naturalness

A teacher who meets new students with ease, whose whole personal appearance speaks of friendliness and warmth, will create an atmosphere of security for his student. The young person who sees the genuineness of such a teacher feels reasonably sure that his personal interests, concerns, and goals are in safe hands. A teacher can, by choosing a relaxed posture and speaking casually and briefly, establish a good relationship with his students at their first meeting.

The first step, then, in getting to know students and their needs is to show that who they are and what they need is of paramount importance in the music program. A teacher who resists the temptation to preach about what he thinks students need and, instead, sits back and lets students reveal their true needs to him is well on the way to success. If he keeps his mouth shut and his eyes open, he can begin to establish mutual acceptance and trust, which open the door to true growth in both teacher and student.

This does not mean that a teacher is gullible. He does not base his music program on fads or the superficial interests of students. However, he investigates student expressions of desired goals and probes the quality and depth of such concerns. After such a search the student, too, will feel reinforced because he will feel he has a partner. After a student accurately perceives his goals, he can embrace the music program, a means to attaining his aims, with enthusiasm.

The teacher's genuineness, his naturalness, creates an inviting atmosphere of learning. Because of their honest realness, both student and teacher can build a trusting relationship which leads to their mutual understanding and appreciation of each other. Because of this trust and acceptance, a student can dare to reach out into new worlds of learning and develop his own initiative and creativity. As their relationship deepens, the teacher builds powers of self-direction and autonomy in the student.

An example of a teacher struggling to learn her students is Anna in the musical *The King and I,* who sings of her experience in the song "Getting to Know You." The song demonstrates the idea that understanding must precede learning. It also explains how judgmental reactions on Anna's part would have inhibited her oriental students from showing themselves and their needs to her.

Look for Nonverbal Messages

Intuition is a shortcut to getting to know students and their needs. By means of intuition a teacher measures students' nonverbal patterns of behavior and reaches "plausible but tentative" judgments without using analytic steps.[1] In other words, the body language of a student gives the teacher a hunch as to who the student is and what kind of learning procedures will fit his needs.

The study of body language, though a relatively new field of research, is a most helpful means of scrutinizing students. The famous psychoanalyst, Alfred Adler, began the practice of observing nonverbal behavior when working with adolescents.[2] He and other psychologists have been able to estimate the kind of personality a student has as well as to predict, to some extent, his future behavior. Because of these studies, teachers today have more information about body language; nevertheless, the observance and interpretation of covert signs and symbols still depends largely on the teacher's powers of intuition.

Eyes are probably the most versatile and efficient data-gathering devices found in nature.[3]

When a teacher meets a student for the first time, their eyes are drawn to study each other's faces. The first encounter with the eyes makes for a significant moment. However, because staring is a violation of privacy, a teacher must observe all he can in unobtrusive glances in which he can note such things about the student as the following.

1. *Notice his body.* Is it too fat? Why? Is it too thin? Rigid? Is he clean? Too clean? Any odor or scent?

2. *Notice how he uses his body.* Are his eyes alive and active? Are they dull, half-closed, or hooded? Does he move them as if he feared danger? Does he have any nervous twitches (tics, blinking, trembling)? Do his fingers seem strong and independent? Does he enjoy color? (Note the clothes he wears.) What is he saying by his posture? Does it suggest that he has a positive idea of himself? Is his walk lazy or energetic, free or rigid, careless or quick? Does he have acne? Asthma? Does he use his eyes, ears, hands, and body when communicating? Is his voice harsh or pleasant? Does he have a musical voice with a variety of pitches? Does he sound angry, contented, or playful? Are his words exact or vague, well-articulated or slovenly? How does he react to you and what you say? Are his gestures those of fear, eagerness, antipathy, or delight? Are his body and bodily coordination sufficiently well developed so as to ensure success in the music program? Do his eyes flit evasively around the room? What does he fix his eyes upon? On the whole, does he seem to be an extrovert or an introvert? Does he seem eager to attach himself to a program and stick with it? Just what do his greatest needs seem to be? Above all, what kind of person does he seem to want to become? Is his self-image low? high? unrealistic? Should he be aiming that high?

Having noted the above, the teacher will be cautious and tentative in his judgments. He must reduce stereotyping to a minimum. Above all, he does well to give the new student a chance to present himself as he really is. The student should feel he is starting anew and his old labels—"lazy," "unreliable," or "slow"—no longer apply.

Prejudicial generalization is a sign of poor education. The educated person has learned to question and search; he does not assume that he already knows.[4]

Listen to the Student by Interviewing Him

Many teachers see their students and interview them in a friendly visit before they make arrangements to accept them into the music program. This interview is a valuable tool with which both student and teacher can assess expectations and likelihood of success in the work they are going to be doing together. Some teachers see their prospective students in May in order to screen their fall classes. Other teachers interview candidates for their programs in order to determine what kind of program the new student will need. Doing this early enables the teacher to search for materials and procedures which will promote optimal growth in a student. The interview is also an opportunity for learning of the unique characteristics of students. It enables the teacher and students to ready themselves for tolerating and reacting to each other's personal traits. The teacher might discuss the following:

Tell me about your family: your mother and father, your place in the family; about your ability to schedule lessons on any day; the possibility of getting help at home; about your parents' plans for you.

Tell me about the selection and amount of music in your home.

Tell me what you think of music. Is it a good beat? Is it a nice tune? Is it a soothing, quiet sound? What kind of music do you want to play? Why do you want to play?

What are your goals for studying music? Do you think you would like to become a professional performer? Are there any serious musicians in your family? Who are your favorite performers?

What can you do with your fingers today? Can you play up and down on the keys, like this . . . ? (Notice physical and motor controls.)

How do you like school? What are your favorite subjects? Do you get average reports? What kind of teacher do you like best?

Do you like sports? Do you play on the team?

Do you have any hobbies?

It is quite impossible to list all the clues to watch for or all the questions to ask. A perceptive teacher formulates questions raised in his mind by nonverbal behavioral cues. He is sensitive to a student's reluctance to answer. He is careful not to overlook significant items which could cause him to miss the very nature of the student's goals in learning. The overall question is, "What does this student need in order to become the person he seems to be forming in himself? How can I help him achieve the skills, understandings, and tastes he is concerned about?"

After assessing the needs of the candidate for the music program, the teacher asks himself, "Am I, as a teacher, capable of giving this person what he needs?" As a rule, a teacher does not accept a student whose needs he cannot meet. Honesty and fairness demand that a teacher refer such a student to other music programs. He makes exceptions to this rule when he is the only person qualified to meet at least some of the needs of such a student.

Why Be Concerned about Needs?

The traditional approach to teaching leads one to believe that the student has but one need—to be taught. Many teachers struggle to provide media and materials in order to tempt the student to think, learn, and relieve his need for knowledge, skill, and understanding. Their attempt, according to Harold Lyon, is to educate the "intellectual half-man."[5] Music teachers train minds, fingers, and voices but quite often neglect the emotional and personal needs of students.

The young person has many basic needs and urges which press for satisfaction. Until these nagging wants are fulfilled, the student cannot dedicate himself to learning. Because he is a human being, a student, too, can rank his needs on Maslow's Ladder of Needs. He craves physical comforts as well as safety and security. Unless these stabilizing human needs are met to some extent, a student does not usually develop a desire for higher-level cognitive skills, aesthetics, or understanding. The following diagram shows how students discussed previously in this book demonstrate their basic needs.

MASLOW'S LADDER AND STUDENT NEEDS*

4. Ego Needs: Ann needs to know that she counts as much as George and others. Phyllis needs to feel that she is a capable, acceptable person.

3. Love and Belonging Needs: David, feeling rejected by his parents and teacher, needs a sense of belonging.

2. Safety, Security Needs: Julie needs the security and safety of the real world before she can relate to it.

1. Physiological Needs: Jerry and his little classmates need bodily movement. Power-hungry George needs physical outlets for his emotions.

Although educators often feel powerless to provide help for a child in his needs, they are usually able to respect the person of the student and help him build his self-image. They can provide, to some extent, a time and place of warmth, acceptance, and loving concern. They will, of course, also learn to know when a student needs the assistance of a professional counselor (or perhaps a doctor) and make the appropriate referral.

In order to provide for the needs of a child, teachers should abandon their patronizing attitudes. Teachers who stoop down in condescending behavior toward students often earn resentment and scorn. On the contrary, teachers who see dignity and worthiness in students win trust and respect. In her writings Maria Montessori

---

* Adapted from Frank Goble, *The Third Force*, p. 52.

95

strongly admonishes her readers never to succumb to the secret urge to think of childrem as empty or bad, as vacuums which need cleaning and filling up. "It is the child who makes the man, and no man exists who was not made by the child who once he was!"[7] Montessori based her reform in education on the nature of man, shown in his capacity to develop freely. A child is not a passive being who owes his life and powers to others; rather, he is an intensely active person who makes himself and his future in response to others. He can fulfill his needs to grow and develop unless his environment frustrates and warps him.

> There is an intimate and necessary relation between the processes of actual experience and education.[8]

Varying Needs of Growing People

Students develop emotionally and intellectually as they meet their needs. Because many students find their environment unsuitable for growing toward maturity, they demonstrate contrasting levels of readiness for learning music.

Some of this variation in readiness is, however, due to age. The paragraphs that follow will treat of the emotional, cognitive, and physical needs unique to students within certain chronological age groups. It should be understood that within such age groups one may find wide variations.

The Needs of the Child from Four to Seven

Emotional Needs. Small children often feel helpless, insecure, and afraid. At times their "why" questions reveal fear of being punished, embarrassed, or hurt. Children ask, "Who played that wrong note?" when they are really asking, "Is it safe to make mistakes here?" Children fear being neglected and abandoned because of their inability to perform like adults. They may fear the ridicule of patronizing remarks such as "pretty good for *you*."

Trying to reason with frightened children is usually the least effective means of reducing fears. However, talking to a child in a supportive, encouraging, and calming way can reduce anxiety and apprehension. One effective technique is that of presenting the fearsome stimulus together with something pleasant, such as candy. A child then experiences the lessening of threat as he enjoys himself.[9]

A teacher can reinforce the confidence of the small child as a person and as a performer by respecting him, his feelings, and his needs. Because a child is empowered by the forces within him to build himself into a man, he deserves respect. In contrast, a teacher who treats a child as a cute plaything is totally unaware of the true powers of a child. To push a child around, to have him "say after me" thousands of meaningless items, or simply to keep him quiet at his desk is demeaning to a child of any age. Yet allowing him to have some autonomy, to make decisions in line with his vision and goals, may seem somewhat threatening for some teachers. Although it involves more work and risk taking to deal respectfully with small children, it is a joyous experience for any teacher to see a human being at work "making himself grow."[10]

The small child feels helpless because he is thwarted repeatedly in his struggle for power or symbols of power. Just as adults experience a need for reputation and importance, children crave some realm, imaginary or actual, where they are kings and queens. By banging a loud triad or playing some noisy drums, a child can experience majestic power. In dance or other rhythmic activities he can feel the power of defying the laws of gravity. Encouraged by an understanding and ingenious teacher, the child can express his power by acting out, singing, playing, or dancing his feelings within a story setting. In the world of make-believe the child is a winner and a hero. He feels safe and important.

The power instinct in children also has its negative aspect, the need to give vent to hostility. At times children's impotence is so painful to them that they desire to strike back and punish those who seem to violate their rights. An example may illustrate this.

One day seven-year-old Raymond, a highly talented student, became extremely angry when I told him that I wanted him to perform in public.

"I won't do it!" His lips were tense, his chin square with anger.

Knowing the changeableness of small children, I was firm but kind. As he put his coat on, I watched him and quietly mused, "Gee, it must be tough—having an old witch like that for a teacher."

He looked up and said softly, "Well, you aren't exactly a witch."

"That's good," I said with a sigh.

"I mean, well, I guess you're more like a frog," he grumbled with disdain.

"Really?" I asked, somewhat stunned.

As I saw the relief in his face, I began to realize that he had felt a need just then to put me down as a slimy creature and step on me. After he had experienced that relief we could laugh, having overcome the heat of our controversy.

Children, even the very young, seem to have an inner radar system with which they quite accurately detect respect and acceptance in adults. For instance, the same child can misbehave in one class, conform in another, and lead the activities in still another, depending upon what elements of safety he detects in the atmosphere of the class and in the attitude and behavior of the teacher.

How can a teacher develop ways of establishing a climate of safety? Certainly it is not by merely acting the role of a "nice" teacher. Rather, it is by developing a deep respect for the child, for his potentiality and his powers. Success with small children depends on a teacher's sincerity as well as his insight. He must know the child in his feelings and his unique ways of thinking and must treat him fairly.

A child feels the need to be loved. In fact, the greatest terror he can have is not being loved.[11] He wants to be treasured, prized, and respected for himself. He abhors and resents, usually, the smothering and coddling which parents and teachers can do so conveniently because of the smallness of his body. He has a very noticeable signaling system to warn a perceptive teacher that this is *not* the time for him to be touched. He responds positively, however, to a teacher who mentions his name often, consults him, asks questions creatively, and gives him the feeling that he is controlling his learning experience to some extent. An effective primary music teacher can be a spark plug at one time, a controlling steering wheel at another, and an energizing motor at still another. For most really significant music experiences, however, the teacher does well to allow the child a certain intimacy with his learning experiences. A teacher who truly loves the child for what he is stands back to some extent and guides the child in his unique way of absorbing and interacting with musical facts, concepts, and skills.

Every child needs to play. His need to play arises not only from his occasional need to escape from adult oppression, but from his natural inclination to imagine and create. A small child does not know the limits of logical thought and so can be far more inventive, expressive, and communicative of his dreams. Although a teacher may try to penetrate a child's playful imaginings, his best efforts usually result only in a confused picture of what the child is experiencing. In the words of the song, "Toyland, Toyland . . . once you pass its borders, you shall never return again." However, a music instructor can feed the play experience. Small children eagerly reach out for rhythmic patterns, chords, melodic sequences, and singsong verses to use as springboards for their creative play.

> As for teaching children concepts that they have
> not yet attained in their spontaneous develop-
> ment, it is completely useless.[12]

Cognitive Needs. Although his emotional framework is similar to that of adults, a small child's cognitive functioning is radically different. Jean Piaget, the Swiss psychologist, found a qualitative difference between the mind of the small child, that of the older child, and that of the adolescent. Small children have, so to speak, their own kind of mental computer with which to process data. For children from four to seven learning is largely knowing how to handle things and taking in information through as many senses as possible. The child wants to reach out to everything, put his hands around things, and bring them to his mouth, eyes, and ears for closer examination and clearer knowledge. He makes trial-and-error adjustments and controls his actions by habit and intuition.

A child learns by doing. After he touches a thing, takes it apart, and puts it together again, he feels he understands it. Music educators who take advantage of children's ability to work by themselves have happier students who learn more readily.

To keep a small child's attention centered on a music task the teacher maintains him on that level in which he attains success. Constant little surprises and new gains excite the child and hold his attention completely. When a child can grasp a thing and move it around, it seems to speak to him and he understands. A preschool child loves to walk on the large music staff lying on the floor and he gets excited when he can make notes go up and down on his favorite toys. A very young child likes to do his work alone and will say such things as "Me do self." Because he likes his own way of doing things, the child can be infuriated by the constant interruption of adults. Usually he tolerates what may seem to him to be stupid adult ways and forgives the people who redo his work according to a mental structure which is totally foreign to him.

Many primary music teachers are frustrated in their work because they think of the child as a miniature adult. They find themselves unable to respect the illogical mind of the child. They wonder why children do not learn the way they "should." Perhaps this statement describing the child mind will demonstrate the child's thinking processes:

The preoperational child is a child of wonder; his cognition appears to be naive, impression-bound and poorly organized. There is an essential freedom in his idea of the world, coupled with an uninhibited zest and excitement with which he approaches new situations. Anything is possible to him because his imagination frees him from lawful constraints.[13]

An insightful teacher knows that logical, rational explanations mean nothing to a child. He knows that highly structured, skill-type approaches do not change the child significantly. As Piaget puts it, ". . . in order to understand we have to invent, or that is, reinvent."[14]

A basic implication in the adult habit of patronizing a child is that the child is less dignified in his thinking structure than the adult. Montessori staunchly defends the power of the child mind. She insists that the child needs this peculiar kind of equipment in order to adjust to life.[15] The adult mind cannot be as open to reality, cannot process the information nor tolerate the abuses which children face. The child mind, therefore, is a fascinating mechanism. It does not operate like an adult mind, but it is no less marvelous than the logical thinking brain. Ginsburg writes, "The child is not just a miniature, although less wise adult, but a being with a distinctive mental structure which is qualitatively different from the adult's. He views the world from a unique perspective."[16]

One example of this unique perspective is the failure to understand principles such as the law of conservation of matter. For small children a quart of water is "more water" when it is divided into several glasses of water. In music class they may believe there are more notes when the symbols are bigger and more widely spaced. For little children logical comparisons, generalizations, and principles are confusing.

Suzuki understood this when he taught children to listen to and copy sounds. He found that the child can take in and process aural stimuli at a surprisingly early age.[17] Linguists believe, too, that children who are learning to talk are extremely perceptive aurally. Carl Seashore believed that talent is inborn and does not vary with age.[18] Perhaps in years to come musicians will make better use of this time of heightened perception in a child's life and further his education by placing more musical stimulation within his experience. More research and experimentation would greatly contribute to this neglected area of music education.

> The child absorbs these impressions not with his
> mind but with his life itself.[19]

Need for Research. How does a small child acquire the concepts and skills of music? Although Piaget discovered a sequential pattern in which a child acquires concepts of space,[20] the natural order of the child's attaining the concepts of sound remains a mystery. Musicians would be richer if Piagetian researchers would investigate and establish the sequence and manner in which children perceive elements of music. A sketchy experiment on rhythm, for instance, suggests that children perceive fast, even rhythmic patterns earlier than slow and uneven patterns.[21] When do children perceive other concepts? How much teaching time is lost when children are told what they already know or what they cannot perceive? The secret of success in teaching is to know the type of process going on in the mind of the child and to direct the educational procedure accordingly.

An example of the uniqueness of a child's perception is his approach to a melody. James Mursell believes that "to a small child, melody is a total contour of tonal movement."[22] The young child does not think of melody as a sequence of separate notes or pitches. The child thinks, instead, in terms of meanings and expressions. He cares little for structure but craves to express his feelings in musical and physical ways.

A teacher whose students are very young has a major responsibility in building a relationship based on mutual trust not only with the child, but with his mother.[23] Maintaining a continuous series of contacts affords the avoidance of teacher-parent conflict as well as the advantage of singlemindedness of approach and appraisal of the child's progress.

Older children who are retarded or deprived can demonstrate

small-child cognitive behavior. Students who have little environmental encouragement to learn may be seriously disinclined to think logically and may prefer the safer way of learning—that of manipulating and handling things.[24]

One resourceful teacher who had a class of restless black youngsters in an inner-city school decided to teach them music through the making of African instruments because the class was still geared to a relatively immature way of learning. This music teacher knew that they would learn about acoustics and the varying pitches of music by putting their hands around an instrument, drawing it to their ears, and feeling that it was their very own. This was a meaningful musical experience which they would remember all their lives. The children not only learned new concepts but began to improve their image of themselves.

Physical Needs. A little child lacks a large, masterful physique with a muscle structure powerful enough to control his instrument. He lacks the lung development to sustain a tone with his breath. Few instruments are really adaptable to the body of a child. Because of this, a small child meets great frustration when he attempts to play an adult instrument. A teacher who has rapport with a student constantly measures not only the child's learning but his frustration, his stress feelings. Stopping before the child has reached his limit of stress may be the saving of a student.

Perhaps the most noticeable need of a child is his need to move. His growing tissues and muscles need the stimulation and circulation which activity brings. This urgency to move does not prevent the mind from functioning unless some authority constrains the child from moving. The emotional conflict within a small child who is forbidden to satisfy his need to move may seriously impede his ability to think or learn.

The Needs of the Child from Eight to Eleven

If he has been given much experience in using his senses to acquire musical concepts, the older child will find himself ready to organize these hazy notions into clear-cut concepts and stable systems of organization.

Considering Seashore's assurance of the child's ability to perceive music stimuli and Piaget's corroboration of the child's ability to conceptualize them, it is evident that a child in the stage of concrete operations is ready to learn concepts of music relationships.[25]

Cognitive Needs. Piaget sees a drastic shift in the quality of mentality in children at the age of seven or eight. Children gradually arrive at the stage at which they perform "concrete operations." That is, so long as children work with concrete objects which they can see and handle, they think rationally and logically. They begin to understand principles and underlying rules and laws such as those of the conservation of matter, gravity, and perspective. Because of this new computer working within them, giving them a new vision of life, children begin a sort of bookkeeping type of learning. These years in his life are a fertile time for the child to stabilize perceptions received previously and to establish precise definitions.

The ability to reason and see relationships begins sometime during these years. Piaget discovered eight "groupings," or kinds of classifications, which children use. He also found that children classify information in only one category at a time.[26] For example, they can organize instruments into classes:

strings + brass + winds + percussion = orchestra

An example may demonstrate the shift in cognitive thinking. Six-year-old Karla looked into my school desk drawer one day and said bluntly, "Oh, what a messy drawer! My mommy makes me clean my drawers when they're messy like that!"

"But, Karla," I said, defending myself, "look—see? The reeds are in this box; the pliers are here; the corks are here. Can't you see that I have good order?"

"You're lucky you don't have my mommy," muttered the outspoken child in utter disgust at my disorderliness. She saw only the great number of materials in a cramped drawer and was unable to see the classification of supplies.

Two years later Karla again looked into the same supply drawer. "You got a lot of stuff in here," she remarked.

"But things are in their place, aren't they?" I asked.

"Yeah, I can see why you find things so fast," admitted Karla, who now knew how to classify and group types of supplies.

The child's cognitive needs lead him to desire to use these newfound ways of coping with reality. He needs much meaningful action. He needs opportunities to process information, and he needs to feel competent. He needs purposeful activities which fit into his frame of reference. Learning theorists have postulated that a student can never take a totally new idea into his mind. All new things must in some way refer to previous learning.[27] Therefore, a student becomes frustrated in music classes and lessons in which he fails to find purpose, relevance, or desirable goals.

During the years between eight and eleven countless children make the serious and lasting decision "Music is not for me." The programs, they decide, are for sissies and snobs. Popular music, which some teachers do not call music, is acceptable to them; but the study and practice of music is, to them, idiotic. What can cause such a conclusion? Probably teachers expect these children to have powers and interests which they do not have.

Because of their being limited to concrete mental functioning, children from eight to eleven usually enjoy charts and factual data. Often such children pride themselves on being too grown-up to believe in fairy tales. They prefer at this stage to hear a brief introduction which does not tell the answers but inspires a "get down to business and find the answer" activity. Their mental equipment at this age is geared to a matter-of-fact approach. Their teacher simply exposes a problem and they set to work.

This is an excellent time for memorizing. Children love their power to lay hold of reality, structure it logically, and keep the information stored. Although this normal process is somewhat tampered with by exposure to television, and although children vary greatly because of emotional differences, usually the memory of a child never works better than when he is in the fifth or sixth grade. At this time he does not yet carry the responsibility older people carry but has excellent mental readiness to classify and retain the concrete world around him.

> It's so much fun to play when you can make the
> music talk!
>
> Liza McCoy (age 9)

Emotional Needs. Although the child from eight to eleven is able to deal objectively and logically with concrete materials, his personal and subjective life is extremely important to him. The people in his life are key factors for him. Trusting relationships with peers, teacher, and parents are vital to his happiness.

Although a child can find great satisfaction in music programs during this stage, he becomes frustrated when teachers expect him to possess an adult mind. Teachers often forget that he cannot reason abstractly, and place before him the task of thinking about future and past and drawing logical conclusions. Although a child dreams of the future, he cannot reason in the future. He cannot address himself to hypothetical thinking, and a teacher's forgetting that makes him restless.

A child may feel angry, too, because teachers seem to be constantly correcting him for his weaknesses. "I hate music," a child will say. Obviously he does not hate music or he would not have delighted in it during previous classes. Rather, he hates the embarrassment of being wrong, the negative feeling of being pushed beyond limits, and the angry feeling of being treated like a thing.

In cases where the child's parents are in music, a child can "hate" music because he feels his parents prefer it to him. He thinks they should spend their time with *him*, not running to concerts, attending rehearsals, or turning the home into a rehearsal studio.

Teachers who are perceptive see these disturbed students and help them find the cause of their negative feelings. If it is failure, the teacher can allow the student to experience feelings of success and well-being.

Some children at this age can develop a fear of difficult material. They want easy music and no challenges. Such problems often seem to dissolve when aired frankly. One might say "Julie, you seem to be afraid . . ." After a sincere discussion of growing just a little bit better through music, a child usually begins to reach out more fearlessly to challenges of ever-increasing proportions.

Because a child can think concretely only, he is unable to cope with generalizations. He is threatened by the vastness of the world of music because it does not reduce itself to his terms. Knowing this, a teacher becomes patient and forbearing with the child who is coping with negative feelings about himself. At this stage the child cannot blame the world for being what it is. He does not always choose to blame music itself or his teacher. Often he simply internalizes the blame and says, "I'm no good." Because this makes him uncomfortable, he can only get relief kicking a stone, making his sister cry, or ruining the music class.

Because a child is capable only of dealing with the here and now, his goals are meaningful only when a clear-cut objective is within sight. Fantasies and dreams are a part of his life, just as they are inherent in human beings at any age. However, abstract and future possibilities seem a bit unreal and do not motivate a growing child as they do a teenager or adult. The young child has to have a goal directly in front of him.

Adults can be really cruel to children by nagging them to learn. Parents tend to fix goals and behavior patterns for children and at times have disagreeable ways of forcing the children to follow those ways.

"Sam doesn't practice unless I make him. Then he doesn't practice well. I want him to . . ." complains a parent.

It does not occur to such a parent that if Sam is capable of deciphering the complex system of notation and mastering embouchure control, he should have the intelligence to know whether he wants to play or what he should do to learn.

This situation can cause much distress and negative feeling about music. It is usually best to come to grips with the problem before it lowers the morale of the whole class or performing unit.

"OK, Sam, either in or out," a teacher can say. "Do you want to play? If you do, you will practice under your own control.

Choose.'' Experience shows that when respected, such a child feels the weight of his responsibility to himself and often chooses to dedicate himself to music. Knowing this, the teacher asks the parent to respect the decision of the student. Since the parent sees that her own way of handling Sam was a failure, she is ready to try anything. This is not the only way to handle apathy in students, but it works in the majority of cases when students are impeded in their progress because of nagging from their parents.

A child like Julie hides her frustration and boredom behind a facade of laziness and ineptness. She dreams during music class and fails to notice much of what goes on around her. She lives in a dream world because she finds no purpose or goal attractive enough to stimulate her enthusiasm. Because she feels that her teachers want to impose irrelevant learning upon her, she dreads such a burden and, so to speak, "plays dead." Julie needs a teacher who, through caring, can reduce her feelings of dread and spark up her enthusiasm. Including names of such children often in classroom talk by saying, "Julie thinks . . . Mary told us . . . See how Jenny played the chord"; seating them in front, looking into their eyes often, and getting them involved physically are all means of helping such withdrawn youngsters become participating members of the class.

For such a child—and, for that matter, normal children—the best teaching is experiential. After a child becomes aware of his experience by touching and feeling, he defines it. Teachers who agree with ancient philosophers that all learning comes through the senses know that teacher talk is an ineffective means of transmitting significant learning. Therefore, a successful teacher is keenly sensitive to the tactile experiences of students. He guides the children as they grasp and grope and try to coordinate their bodies. Above all, he leads the children to be close to their experience and he frees them for creativity. As Piaget says, "Every time you teach a child something you keep him from re-inventing it."[28] Teachers do well to build students up by allowing them to know themselves and develop their own frame of reference.

Often children are not in touch with their feelings. Teachers can, at times, guess what children feel and can aid them either to talk, sing, or play it out or express their feelings by other physical responses. In hurried classroom situations as well as at private lessons, there is little time to talk about feelings. Teachers, however, can usually detect strong feelings in a child and deal with them indirectly. For example, one could say, "Supposing, class, that someone had just been unfair to us and we feel like getting even, how do you suggest we play that chord to express it? Could you show me how you would play it if you felt like socking a mean guy?" Students feel relieved. They show noticeable relaxation and often laugh after they release their anger.

Physical Needs. Teachers who are cognizant of the physical needs of growing children can use the medium of music to fulfill them. Boys, especially, often need vibration and high intensities of volume to satisfy their need for movement. The child of ten often feels a sudden development in his fingers and muscular structure. This tingling in his fingers makes him crave manipulative outlets. "I want to play!" he hears his muscles saying. Therefore, he reaches out more enthusiastically for procedures which are practical and active rather than theoretical. He is eager to "run" up and down the keys, he wants to "punch" the chord, and he desires the effective use of his muscles.

It is good to remember that, if permitted, the child in this age category is alert enough to manage his own affairs. However, because he cannot manage abstract data, he feels forced into conformity with what adults ask of him. He seeks autonomy and respect. He experiences a growing discontent in being referred to as a child. He takes on a natural sophistication and says, "I'm not a little kid anymore!"

> An adolescent who has adapted too well in his role as a child and has become too comfortable with it finds it difficult to assume his new role as an adult.[29]

According to Piaget's theory, the final period of cognitive development in a person, the "formal operations level," takes place at about the age of twelve. This final shift in the quality of thinking, coming as it does, at about the time of puberty, brings about more emotional upheaval than previous changes. Because their emotionality is so intense and unpredictable, teenagers tend to threaten their teachers. Yet the energy, the beauty, and potential of youth effectively attract teachers to dedicate themselves to finding and fulfilling the needs of tomorrow's adults. Teaching teenagers is at once stimulating and self-enriching for any music teacher.

Cognitive Needs. Before twelve the child's quality of thinking is oriented to the here-and-now solving of concrete problems, organizing and classifying data, and believing all adult formulations. The teenager's mind begins to be flexible. A new power to think hypothetically, an ability to think in the abstract, as well as a lively zest for problem solving and creative choosing begin to enrich the youth. Powers of intuition and the ability to appreciate aesthetic beauty begin to heighten in adolescence.

Effects of Cognitive Change. The shift to the stage of formal operations plays a critical role in a student's adjustment. The new acquisition of hypothetical thinking ability leads the teenager to become aware of the discrepancy between the actual state of affairs and the possible remedies about which he can theorize. He begins to question the values of teachers and parents and freely rebels when he believes that adults do not "practice what they preach." He becomes angry with himself for having been gullible during childhood and having allowed himself to be enslaved by authority. Now he takes revenge by being reckless and noncomforming.

David at seventeen plays his Beethoven sonata lustily and yet with gentle feeling. In his uniqueness, however, he builds his phrases and suddenly dimishes just where I expect him to finish his crescendo.

"But, David, I disagree. Look, here is the punch word in that musical sentence," I say as I mark an X over the climactic note of the phrase. "Can't you see that, David?"

Of course, David sees the logic of my reasoning. Yet somehow he likes being different. Why should he place his emphasis on the same note that has been stressed for years? By playing softly when others expect him to accent a note, David is showing himself to be master of his world, an innovative and creative young man. When he no longer feels the need to be different and develops a respect for his craft, he may come back to find and honor the X's in his music.

Because of his new powers and creative problem-solving ability, a student such as David wants to try new effects and combinations. Although teachers are often conventional in their tastes, students, on the contrary, find tremendous pleasure and fascination in new combinations in music, in new sounds, and in new procedures. The "sky is the limit" to the imagination of a teenager. Students feel a need for freedom in experimenting. Any teacher who sharply rebukes a student for "wrong" methods may have trouble working with teenagers. Is there any known "right way"? Who has ever formulated the one-to-one correlation between the digital and muscular action of a performer and the "right" sound of a masterwork?

Emotional Needs. Adolescents also show their development in new attitudes toward themselves. Because they can reason hypothetically, they use their new powers to become analytical and introspective.[30] At times they can discuss and engage in highly impersonal debate on philosophical topics. At other times they become egocentric and self-conscious, thinking that the whole world is looking at their big feet, large noses, clumsy hands.

Teenagers suddenly awaken from their childhood "unthinking conformity" and ask, "Why do I let people push me around?" They begin to develop a keen sensitivity which detects the slightest violation of their integrity. They may ferret out the peeves of teachers and use every opportunity to "pay them back" for the authoritarian rule of their childhood. If possible, they wear the wrong clothes, come in at the wrong hours, and disregard those social conventions which adults expect them to uphold. As Ginott states,

> The purpose of adolescence is to loosen personality. . . . Personality is undergoing the required changes: From organization (childhood) to disorganization (adolescence) to reorganization (adulthood). Adolescence is a period of curative madness, in which every teenager has to remake his personality. He has to free himself from childhood ties with parents, establish new identifications with peers, and find his own identity.[31]

The greatest emotional need of the teenager is acceptance. At no time in his life is his sense of identity so fluid as in adolescence. The boy or girl is no longer a child, but surely cannot be accepted as an adult. He or she feels a constant change in personality as well as bodily feelings and because they do not know how to cope with these, they puzzle and confuse those around them with most inconsistent behavior. The music teacher who succeeds with young people sees deeper than the superficial shifts in youth. He accepts the student as a person, a respectable human being, even when he is floundering with new powers awakening within him.

First, the teacher shows respect for the teenager. Then he guides the student to respect and accept himself. In building this self-acceptance within the student, the teacher carefully avoids preaching or referring to his own youth. "When I was your age . . ." is a phrase which enrages and deafens a teenager. Often an adult does not know, really, what a teenager experiences; nor does he know how to advise him. The best he can do is respect him and empathize to the very highest degree. The teacher can listen and help the student build himself. He can assist a student in being objective and in outlining his priorities; he can guide him indirectly in making good choices. A wise teacher refrains from making decisions for students.

When a music teacher notices the problem of a lack of security in a student, he tries to help the student by showing warmth and acceptance. Allen, a perfectionistic tenor who overworks to get his notes, needs to be praised for his personal values and his unique personal characteristics, not only for his superior singing. Calling

Allen by name, perhaps even by a nickname (rather than, "Hey, you, the tenor in the middle!") is a person-building technique. Allen needs to feel that it is safe to be one's natural self here in choir. He is more than a good tenor. He is a great young man in the process of becoming even greater. When he begins to realize that, his singing will improve, too.

Some students try to solve their insecurity problems by identifying with one adult. They lean on this person, imitating his behavior and taking on his attitudes. This parasitic practice seriously impedes maturity in both student and teacher. Music instructors who find themselves victims of teenage adulation often feel complimented by the attention given them. The professional person, hungry for ego-satisfaction, can foster the process and encourage it. However, since such love is really a "cop-out" for the courageous facing of a student's true growth needs, it is disastrous for both student and teacher. A truly genuine teacher is quick to notice slavish imitative conduct.

Confusion about personal identity may cause teenagers to become egocentric and self-conscious. It is not uncommon for a student of twelve or older to become completely overcome with anxiety before a public performance. At the age of six Jennie played with the utmost pride. Now, at twelve, she feels others are analyzing and judging her as a person and a performer. Overcome with overwhelming fear, Jennie cries, "Oh, I can't! I'm not ready!"

Other adolescents use music as a cushion and a protection from their uncomfortable introspective thoughts. A pianist may tend to play overly loud and keep his foot on the pedal constantly. Repeated admonitions by his teacher remain unheard. Suddenly, as he begins to feel more fulfilled, his pedal habits return to normalcy. Instrumentalists and singers may want to perform extremely fast or rhythmically. Nonperformers often turn radios and phonographs to high-decibel levels in order to create the illusion that they are not alone with themselves.

When misunderstanding and alienation mount in his life a teenager often becomes furiously angry. Reluctant to expose such angers openly, he feels a "cold war" inside him. His subtle way of annoying the teacher, however, sets off the fires of anger in him, too. Now there is open battle. An honest, genuine teacher who knows he accepts the student as a respectable person, can attack the situation, not the personality of the student. He can say, "OK, Scott, the valve oil is spilled: wipe it up." When Scott is alone with the teacher afterwards, he can tell the whole story of why he deliberately spilled the oil to anger the teacher. When he sees a teacher who can respect him even when he makes bad choices, he finds better ways of solving his personal problems. As he learns to take responsibility for his actions, the margin of error and poor judgment grows smaller—little by little.

Because a young person is psychologically set to act in a certain manner but is prevented from doing what he wants, he becomes angry. How does a teacher deal with anger? First of all, a teacher does well to meet it patiently, without surprise. To reduce the heat of the anger, the teacher does all he can not to become also inflamed with anger. If the teacher listens respectfully, the evident loving attention to the person often placates the student. Above all, it is well to remember that youths have great resiliency. Their moods and emotions can shift readily. A successful teacher relaxes, accepts them as they are, hopes for the best, and usually finds the students giving their best.

Teenagers suffer from fear. The sources of their fear, lack of clear notions about personal identity and lack of security, are easier to cite than to resolve. One core remedy for fear is to replace it with success. Clear up his concepts. Let him tell things as he sees them. Assure him before performing by setting a slow but enjoyable tempo. When he is ill with fear, ask easy questions or play for him. In sum, the solution is to allay fears by putting the student into a situation where no threat is possible.

Teenagers are often busy and frustrated people. When an adolescent finds his burden too heavy to bear, it is good for a music teacher to sit down with him and honestly discuss his goals. What is he aiming at? Is he going at it in the right way? Are there varying levels of assignments so that sometimes the student is challenged, at others easily successful? Does the teacher take his share of the blame for failures in realistic goal making?

The teacher of adolescents has the advantage of working with very "alive" people. With the flow of sexual hormones into his body, a new energy, a new vitality, enlivens the whole spirit of youth. Freed from the narrowness of childhood thinking, he now has both the cognitive and physical power to be enterprising and adventurous. He feels he can and must remake the world.

The thirst for power is strong in the adolescent. Feeling impotent because of his slavery as a student and his dependence at home, a student can find tremendous releases for power in music. Teachers who are constantly alert to the students' need for expressing power save themselves much trouble. A student can feel power when he helps shape class procedures or decides what music he will study. He can release his drive for power by playing stormy passages with vehemence and drive. At another time he can play softly and intimately, withholding his tone, and thereby showing his power. Music teachers who empathize with students and use music to develop maturity and growth are successful in many dimensions.

One quality of teenagers which is often ignored in teaching practices is their love for ecstasy and exotic beauty. Because of the hurried pace of classes and lessons, teachers tend to develop only the most superficial level of the teenager's talent. However, young people crave ecstatic experiences. They want to *be* music and let the flow of their phrases be the very breathing of their souls. They often feel frustrated when teachers train them to be mere finger-pushers and mechanical dwarfs. They feel music is irrelevant if it does not express the vibrancy of human life within them.

Above all, teenagers crave stability. Though they want to be respected as freewheeling and autonomous, they seek to know standard and accepted ways in which they can feel secure. After a student sees and experiences the traditional interpretation and dynamism of a piece, he likes being allowed to deviate from this. Teachers can successfully allow freedom of interpretation by asking the student to defend his choices. His new "If . . . then" type of thinking seeks experience in dealing with factors of music.

In a secure framework, he makes safe choices and still is very close to being "right." A very deep need of every teenager is to become an adult who is acceptable and successful.

> Relationships with adults nevertheless are also perceived as potentially dangerous. This is due to a fear of losing one's individuality and identity.[32]

Peer Group Influence

Although teenagers outwardly conform to some norms, they cleave to their peers for understanding and sympathy. The support of adults has been seriously lessened. With the loosening of ties between adolescents and their parents, the bonds between peers become tighter. Young people need to share their strong and often confusing feelings, their doubts, their dreams, and their ideas. Because their peers have as many or more personal problems, most teenagers feel less threatened when they associate with people their own age.

Young people interact with each other in ways geared to win mutual acceptance from each other. They feel an urge to learn each other's problems and try to solve them. They crave praise, enrichment, and support from others their own age.

Music teachers who know the tenacity of these relationships can reap a rich harvest of success by utilizing peer group pressures. By getting students to stimulate a nonachieving member of the class, teachers implement the strongest motivational forces possible. Wise teachers know that students willingly change when peers step in. Class piano teachers find that students feel enriched by group repertoire and idea exchange classes. They even consider such events as high spots of the week.[33]

Some practical methods of utilizing peer interaction are (1) telling a student to ask a peer for a fingering, an interpretation, or an explanation; (2) seating a languid or slow student next to a capable helper; (3) introducing procedures with words such as,

"Carrie likes to do it this way . . ." or "Sally tells us that . . .";
(4) giving teenage analogies ("Like the pushing of a bicycle"); (5)
giving solutions of some students as options for others ("Marvin
found that he had to use two hands here.")

The Adult Student

Whether an adult sings or performs, his head is usually easier to
teach than his body. Teaching adults differs from the teaching of
young people in these ways: (1) Adults are highly motivated. (2)
They are less regular, having other responsibilities. (3) They can
perform but are constantly frustrated by their lack of muscular
coordination. (4) They are impatient and easily embarrassed. (5)
They are more willing to drill and do exercises than teenagers. (6)
They seek the security of counting aloud or other means of making
sure they are right. (7) They want to learn correctly.

Although adults are different in outlook, teachers find them enjoyable as students. Eager and hard-working, they tend to like their
instructors for the very qualities for which young people despise
them. Teachers who include some adults in their schedules add interest and variety to their professional lives. They can share experiences which, though perhaps only peripherally related to music,
engender a feeling of camaraderie between adult student and
teacher.

Principles of Meeting Needs

The study of student needs covers a vast field. Yet there are three
general principles that may aid in implementing student-centered
music programs. The first principle is that a child is not a small-
sized and less wise adult. The growing child acquires a series of different cognitive computers, so to speak, with which he deals with
learning tasks. He abandons less effective thinking patterns as he
reaches higher stages of cognitive and emotional development.
Teachers often completely fail to see the child's perspective, chaotic
and illogical as it may be, and fail also to bring him just a little

117

closer to intellectual maturity. Educators must be more sensitive to and perceptive to the cognitive development of each child, and must allow the child freedom to manipulate, organize, and create in order to heighten his mental functioning.

Secondly, the major source of learning is activity—either physical or conceptual. The child or youth needs to interact with his learning in, at least, a partially self-directed way. He must be allowed to manipulate articles or notes—seeing, hearing, feeling, and touching musical data. At all times, the child must be active, reinventing things for himself.

Finally, implementing a program directed to the satisfaction of student needs is both important and urgent. Music teachers, in becoming specialists, have all too often focused their attention on the literature which they wish to teach and have seriously neglected the frame of reference and ability of the student. Through sensitivity and awareness of student needs and goals, the music teacher can find a new framework and focus for his programs as well as increased success in his attempts to teach. When students experience significant learning, their music lessons are times of personal and musical growth and fulfillment.

Notes

1. Jerome S. Bruner, *The Process of Education* (New York: Random House, Vintage Books, 1960), p. 13.

2. Donald H. Clark and Asya L. Kadis, *Humanistic Teaching* (Columbus, Ohio: Charles E. Merrill Publishing Co., 1971), p. 16.

3. James J. Thompson, *Beyond Words,* p. 93.

4. Donald H. Clark and Asya L. Kadis, *Humanistic Teaching,* p. 130.

5. Harold D. Lyon, Jr., *Learning to Feel—Feeling to Learn,* p. 35.

6. Adapted from Frank Goble, *The Third Force,* p. 52.

7. Maria Montessori, *The Absorbent Mind* (New York: Dell Publishing Co., 1967), p. 15.

8. John Dewey, *Experience and Education* (New York: Macmillan Publishing Co., 1938), p. 7.

9. Paul Henry Mussen, John Janeway Conger, and Jerome Kagan, *Child Development and Personality* (New York: Harper & Row, Publishers, 1974), p. 389.

10. Maria Montessori, *The Secret of Childhood* (New York: Ballantine Books, 1966), p. 30.

11. John Steinbeck, *East of Eden,* pp. 170-1.

12. Jean Piaget as quoted in Elizabeth Hall, "A Conversation with Jean Piaget and Barbel Inhelder," *Psychology Today* IV (May 1970), 30.

13. Sr. Cecilia Schmitt, "The Thought Life of the Young Child," *Music Educators Journal* 58 (December 1971), 24.

14. Jean Piaget quoted in F. G. Jennings, "Jean Piaget: Notes on Learning," *Saturday Review* XLIX (May 20, 1967), 81.

15. Maria Montessori, *The Absorbent Mind,* p. 25.

16. Herbert Ginsberg and Sylvia Opper, *Piaget's Theory of Intellectual Development* (Englewood Cliffs, N.J.: Prentice-Hall, 1969), p. 219.

17. Shin'ichi Suzuki, *Nurtured by Love* (New York: Exposition Press, 1969).

18. Carl Seashore, *Psychology of Music* (New York: McGraw-Hill Book Co., 1938), p. 3.

19. Maria Montessori, *The Absorbent Mind,* p. 24.

20. Jean Piaget, *The Child's Conception of Space* (New York: Norton Library, 1967).

21. Sr. Cecilia Schmitt, "A Paradigm of Music Concepts" (unpublished master's thesis, University of Minnesota, 1971), p. 40.

22. James Mursell, *The Psychology of Music* (New York: W. W. Norton and Co., 1937), p. 101.

23. Paul Henry Mussen and others, *Child Development and Personality,* p. 353.

24. Gerald Weinstein and Mario D. Fantini, eds., *Toward Humanistic Education: A Curriculum of Affect* (New York: Praeger Publishers, 1970), p. 21.

25. Robert J. Neidlinger, "Dimensions of Sound and Silence," *Music Educators Journal* 59 (April 1973), 29.

26. For a detailed explanation see: J. H. Flavell, *The Developmental Psychology of Jean Piaget* (Princeton, N.J.: D. Van Nostrand Co., 1962), pp. 186-201.

27. Donald Snygg, "The Psychological Basis of Human Values," *The Helping Relationship Sourcebook* (Boston: Allyn & Bacon, 1971), p. 103.

28. Jean Piaget, as quoted by F. G. Jennings, "Jean Piaget: Notes on Learning," p. 83.

29. Committee on Adolescence, *Normal Adolescence* (New York: Charles Scribner's Sons, 1968), p. 44.

30. Paul Henry Mussen and others, *Child Development and Personality,* p. 554.

31. Haim G. Ginott, *Parent and Teenager* (New York: Avon Books, 1969), p. 25.

32. Committee on Adolescence, *Normal Adolescence,* p. 67.

33. Ylda Novik, "Teaching Teens in the Weekly Piano Class," *Clavier* XII (January 1973), 35.

5

Special Types of Rapport

A man who cannot relate is a failure no matter
what his talents are.

Can All People Relate?

Every person has an organic urge to relate to others.[1] This basic
need carries with it an innate ability every person has to live as a
social human being. Therefore, it is safe to assume that every music
teacher can establish rapport with his students. It is also clear that
students have the right to expect their teachers to relate
meaningfully to them. No one, teacher or student, can grow to personal or musical maturity unless others relate to him in a human
way. Yet, it is true that many teachers fail to establish good
relations with students. They fail partially as music educators
because they neglect to find out just who the students are
emotionally, intellectually, and musically. Part of this neglect
results from the lack of explicit stress on human relations in teacher
training sessions or seminars in music education.

Although the focus of attention in many music education settings
is currently still on performance,[2] no teacher succeeds without
some ability to interact with students. Many educators do not
bother to respect their students; yet they do, at least, meet student
expectations for efficient, reliable instruction and exciting class ac-

tivities. The teacher who is in rapport with his students not only knows how to keep the classes moving, but knows his students as individuals. He not only aims at high standards of achievement in music, but he designs music activities which are appropriate to his particular students.

Because through close interaction a teacher meets different needs in different situations, his behavior varies greatly. A judicious teacher ponders carefully just what kind of interrelationship is needed in a certain circumstance and he carefully fosters the behavior which will give him optimum success.

> As a teacher I am an available resource with the patience to let it happen. Then students can bring about their own self-fulfilling prophecies of loving and learning. I act in spite of the complexity, the mystery, and the threat of existential reality.[3]

Classroom Rapport and One-to-One Rapport

What is the difference between classroom rapport and private-lesson rapport? How much rapport is possible in teaching situations where large numbers of students meet with a teacher? Is rapport possible in all circumstances?

First of all, good interpersonal relations depend upon the *willingness* of persons to relate. Rapport does not depend on the size of the room or how many people are in it. Two people must see some advantage in associating with each other. This relationship can be deep or shallow, warm or cool, but its power to influence the two people involved depends entirely upon how much they want to relate to one another.

Rapport remains superficial when an instructor centers the class or lesson on music literature rather than on the needs of the student. In such instances, although the student voices his personal opinions at times, the teacher's attention stays on the music, not on the student. However, even in the most businesslike atmosphere, a certain degree of rapport is necessary in order to hold a class together. Usually a conductor shows personal favor to those who work hardest and excel in classwork. These students he honors by giving them leadership positions and a certain amount of personal warmth. They, in turn, exert power over their peer group and often work to unify the group and stimulate its response to the teacher whom they love. These moves and relationships are subtle, however, and teacher and student are only dimly conscious of the casual procedures.

Because of the uniqueness of each student, teachers relate to individual students, not to groups. Although a teacher can love a group for its general atmosphere and cooperation, this relating is not really deep or lasting. A person who relates well sees in his class a mosaic of individuals, each special in his own way. As these music students enter or leave class, he relates to them, speaking personally to each one. During class he carefully notes the failures, frustrations, successes and achievements of each person and watches individual reactions to his teaching procedures. He also chats personally when he tests voices, repairs instruments, or assembles equipment.

Private lessons are excellent opportunities for developing rapport. In schools where instrumentalists can meet with their teacher regularly, they sometimes develop a keenly sensitive relationship. Instrumental or vocal students who study privately experience the full attention of a teacher who can build a music study program completely around their needs, goals, and limitations. At times the relationships of these private lessons become so close that the students identify with the teacher, taking on his patterns of thought and behavior. On the other hand, when the teacher cannot relate to a student's need, when he is impatient with the student, or when he is somewhat threatening or boring, the students often discontinue lessons. Private students expect a higher degree of rapport with their teachers than classroom students do. To many private students it is intolerable to be alone with an adult for an hour or a half hour each week when they cannot relate meaningfully to that person.

Whether a teacher is relating to a person in class or in a private lesson, he develops the kind of rapport he desires; relating to students is a behavior which a teacher chooses. To begin, a teacher must be open and honest to his students and accept them as they are. He must respect students as free human beings with personal dignity. Circumstances and personalities can hinder relationships, but only stubbornness can prevent them.

Teacher-Parent Rapport

The rapport of a teacher with each of his students' parents is greatly important. That teachers need parental support in developing and maintaining music programs is obvious. Yet it is also true that many teachers are fearful, critical, and even hostile to parents with whom they have a common bond.

Teaching is not a one-way street. Teachers not only give information; they need to receive some, too. They need to sit down with parents and honestly search for ways in which they, as teachers, have initiated problems or allowed them to develop. How did his student, their child, get those inferiority feelings? Did the teacher constantly demand that he do work that he could not do? Why did he lose his good self-image? Did adults fail to listen to him, respect him, love him?

Discussions are most effective when teachers and parents are fair and objective. "Sammy does grab things away from others during class," a teacher may say. "I feel that he craves my attention, and he knows how I hate that and will notice him when he does it." Does the teacher condemn Sammy? No, he must have a reason for his actions. Because his parents and teachers now know that what Sammy is really seeking—love and acceptance—is rightfully his, they can fulfill his needs and dissolve the problem little by little.

Another teacher, however, may tell the parents an exaggerated story of Sammy's classroom rudeness and incriminate the boy with negative or false charges. The parents, in turn, can become infuriated and withdraw the child from the music class. They may even succeed in crippling the entire music program of that teacher.

Teachers should keep their interviews with parents personal and positive. "Sara is most adept at clapping rhythms," a primary teacher may say. "She is not, unfortunately, able to stop her clapping at the right time." In this way the teacher emphasizes the power of the child and works from there to weaker areas. Such an approach is assuring to an adult who fears the blame which teachers can so easily project on them or their children. "I can't help getting a bit ruffled, Mrs. Stone," admits the teacher, "when Sara keeps clapping when I want her to be quiet." After this the mother may admit that Sara definitely needs self-discipline and she, as parent, has not been helpful enough in teaching her to develop it. By admitting their shortcomings, this teacher and mother resolve not only to help the child, but to improve their own behavior.

Some successful teachers rarely confer with parents. They see the child and use the imaginary visit of the parent as a means of stimulating the child to direct himself in remedying the situation. "Pat, I told you last week that you must not forget your music again. Do I have to talk to your mother?" a teacher may ask.

"No, I'll never forget it again, I promise," Pat assures his teacher.

"You know how I hate to bother your mom with business which really is yours and mine. Let's keep our music problems just between us, huh?" confides the teacher.

This "just between you and me" approach is extremely effective. A child of seven or eight often shows visible signs of feeling, "Aha, I'm finally a man." The strong forces of personhood within each child or youth can effectively change a thoughtless youngster into a responsible student.

Yet it is true that parent-teacher conferences are necessary at times. A teacher does well to recall his own values in dealing with students before he meets parents. He can renew within his mind his determination to be respectful, trusting, and concerned, but not possessive. He remembers how he believes in his students' potential and is concerned about their growth. His aims are to empathize with students and be relevant to them. He wants to provide for the students a safe, structured, but free classroom or studio atmosphere.

Sometimes a teacher is so highly regarded that parents come to him seeking advice for themselves. It is not a good policy, however, for a teacher to give definite answers or make decisions for other people. Usually it is best to listen empathically and ask thought-provoking questions which lead the advice seeker to discover his priorities and solve his own problem.

Many times after a good conversation with a parent, a teacher may come to realize that parents are education's most neglected resource. The rapport and friendship between parents and teachers can become a major boost for the entire music program. Teachers who take parents just as they are, patiently show human acceptance and understanding, and are able to join with the parents in loving the child wisely, begin to feel a firm support in a joint relationship with parents. Little by little, through the parents' greater interest and concern for the values and goals of the program, the teacher-parent-student rapport stimulates the kind of vitality which, in turn, begins to produce successful results.

> There is no such thing as a problem child. . . .
> Pinning on him such a label too often adds still
> another burden. . . .
>
> Every problem, like its owner, is unique, and the
> solution must be unique.[4]

DEALING WITH SPECIAL PROBLEMS

For some students a competent teacher who has a friendly, real smile is adequate. Other students make heavier demands. They call out for sympathy, love, and freedom. Some are restless because they have gifts which no one sees or helps them develop. Such students seek someone who will take time to notice them, encourage them, and listen to them. They need, above all, to develop a trusting relationship with someone in order to break down the obstacles to learning which they experience within themselves. The scared learner, the hostile or discouraged pupil, is always a poor learner because he scatters his emotional and cognitive forces in battling on two fronts.

The Shy Student

Reuben was a shy boy, unable to act spontaneously. He became tense and uptight the minute he entered the band room. My aim was to make him more self-confident. He needed a learning situation which was supportive of his growing happiness with himself. I knew that I, his teacher, must provide a tone of acceptance which his classmates would also adopt. As he sat down, I let him know quietly and unobtrusively that I was pleased to have him with me in class. I reassured him by kind glances, smiles, or by putting my hand gently on his shoulder now and then. Gradually, my patience and belief in him were repaid by his increasing trust in himself, in me, and in the other band members.

There were two precautions I took with Reuben. First, I did not violate his "private space" and was sure that he did not feel threatened when I came too close to him or touched him. After he began to trust me and value me as a person and as a helper in building himself, he overcame his shyness in class.

The other precaution I took flowed from the first. I was careful not to ruin my program of person building by expecting unrealistic achievements or by asking him to play difficult material alone in class or in public. Reuben experienced confidence when the stakes were low. Had I pressed this shy child too hard, I could have lost him.

> Learning is the discovery that something is possible.[5]

The Tense Student

Her brow wrinkled with anxiety and her hands fumbling with the buttons of her coat, Millie came in to her piano lesson. My first task was to try to put her at ease and free her, as much as I could, from those pent-up worries with which she seemed to be bothered. I was determined to break down that tenseness. I decided to try to get her to express her feelings in the here and now both in words and through the performing of music.

"Have trouble getting here?" I asked, trying to free her by focusing on travel problems.

"Yeah, darn train came through . . ."

"Yes, I stood at the crossing a long time myself today. Now, let's have a good lesson."

"Oh, it's gonna be terrible. I didn't practice . . . had a big test."

"Too bad. Say, is that the Chopin *Scherzo* here in your stack of music? Must have been scary getting started on that at first!"

"Yeah, well, maybe I should have tried . . ."

It became apparent that Millie's fears and apprehension were the obstacles which were keeping her from learning. The sooner she and I acknowledged and remedied this problem, the sooner she could courageously take on more challenging work. By being open about the fear of difficulty and balancing it with words of confidence, the teacher can help the student to grow in self-confidence.

The most devastating approach to allaying fears and tense feelings is to deny them. A teacher could have told Millie, "Oh, you shouldn't be nervous. This is really easy to do. See . . . ?" Such a statement blames Millie for her fears. It embarrasses her and makes her feel silly by demonstrating that the music she fears is so simple that it is not worth working for.

Therapeutic antidotes for tension are physical releases such as pounding, hitting, screaming, jumping, or crying. Since music studios are somewhat private, it is possible at times to work out severe tensions in these ways. However, because students are expected to learn how to perform during lessons and classes, it is best to release the tension through musical expression.

All students, even beginners, can experience a release of tension and can express personal power by playing loudly in many registers. Running up and down the scales can give the illusion of escaping and running away. Intermediate students can find a feeling of masterfulness which is tension-releasing in playing with greater intensity, greater speed, or more varied contrast. Any music that has sudden sforzando effects or climaxes tends to give the "I've got you at my mercy" feeling. With a bit of coaching in this use of it, students can use music to become more positive, balanced persons.

Sometimes students are tense because the teacher who pretends to accept them betrays his underlying annoyance by constant nagging and criticism. Students who tense up unreasonably just before music sessions can defeat their purpose of trying to advance in music unless they are able to discuss the problem with their teacher. It is obviously the teacher who should initiate such a discussion. Though neither one may know exactly where to start in trying to solve the problem of tension, the teacher cannot wrong a student by telling him simply that he is concerned about his uneasiness. Even if a student does not, perhaps cannot, share his deep fears with the teacher, such encounters usually improve conditions as time goes on.

Music is heightened speech—Music begins
where speech lets off.[6]

The Verbally Inept Child

Max was a boy who talked little. At first I thought he was shy; but as I worked with him, I noticed that he was not afraid. Rather, he was innately empowered to speak more with his fingers than with his tongue.

My approach to his organ study became mainly that of music communication. For Max, the organ sang like a bird, lulled one to sleep, raged angrily, spoke tender messages of love. The organ communicated all that Max needed to say but could never find the words for.

To some extent every talented musician is unable to talk as well as he can speak through his singing or the extension of his body, his musical instrument. Max, however, would have become extremely dwarfed in his emotional growth if we had not discovered his urgent need for the communicative powers of music.

129

One day Laura stayed after a choral rehearsal to complain of her problems. "I guess I just get mad too easily. You know, don't you, that I was rejected by my parents when I was a baby?" It was the whine of a dejected teenager. I could see that she was not alert to all the love and attention which her foster parents and others were trying to show her in the here and now. She had too much pent-up hostility for her parents to be able to appreciate or even see reality.

"You would really like to pay them back for rejecting you, wouldn't you, Laura?" I asked.

"Just think of how they must have hated me! I must have been ugly and bothersome to them. I wish I could tell them," confided the girl as the pain of these dark thoughts clouded her face.

"Well, Laura, maybe you can tell them. Maybe they will hear you by ESP sometime," I suggested. "Here, let's sing about it," I proposed as I pulled out some soul-stirring spirituals. Laura took an old bell off the piano and used it as an imaginary microphone which supposedly would carry as far as her parents' ears. She sang with all the emotion her small body contained. She also sang some hard rock and stamped the floor, punishing her parents in effigy.

After Laura had worn herself out singing, she felt quite relieved of her resentment. She smiled and seemed quite in touch with the realization that, although her parents had placed her in another home when she was a baby, she was a lucky girl to have so many lovely friends and concerned adults caring for her.

Many music teachers would have discounted Laura's problems. They would have said that she had no reason for her hostility and was probably just "putting it on." Too few teachers know how to use music to heal distressed people.

They trust in me and this trust is more powerful
than steel.

The Deprived Student

Who is deprived? Although the meaning of the word *deprived* is often limited to those experiencing financial poverty, anyone who is hindered in growth is deprived. Lynn, for instance, is a rich young lad who sits in band playing a $700 Selmer clarinet. Lynn has all the money he can use; but it does not buy him care, understanding, and safety. Because Lynn is deprived of some of his most basic needs, he is angry, restless, hostile. His most basic needs and rights as a human being are being withheld from him.

Adults can be blind to a child's need for love. It is common for teachers to scorn the deprived child who presses for safety, admiration, notice, and love. "Stop showing off, Sara," a teacher says. In this way he refuses to give Sara the care and respect of which she feels deprived already. Certainly it is not commendable to foster attention-getting behavior. However, class-disturbing is a symptom of something much deeper and it is the teacher's responsibility to contribute to the fulfillment of the needs of his students, needs which must be identified.

Nancy, financially and culturally deprived, has her own style of learning. Because she is an inner-city student raised in squalor, she rejects logical methods in favor of more kinesthetic, manipulative procedures. She tells her teacher, "Let me do it. I want to make it work." She wants to hold the instrument, feel it, lay hold of its secrets through her hands rather than through the verbal and rational sequences dictated by her teacher.

Can a teacher empathize with the deprived? Does a teacher himself experience any deprivations? All people, including teachers, are needy. When a teacher admits this to a student, together they become conscious of a deeper respect for themselves and a greater acceptance of the problems shared by all simply because they are human.

> The Navajo language has ten words meaning honor; it has as many denoting respect. Why do we have so few?

The Handicapped Child

Jean, fourteen, stood with her mother in the doorway of my studio. When I glanced up, her mother said, "Jean, here, would like to learn piano, I mean, if you'll have her."

I walked toward her and assured her that music would be great fun for her and I would enjoy having her. I slowly estimated her assets and inabilities. Her hands were large and strong. Her eyes were poor, and her speech was indistinct. My estimation of Jean's ability that first day proved to be quite accurate. She did have a good ear and a strong hand. Her reading was poor; but, though her reasoning power was dim, she could memorize some notes and could remember finger and notational patterns accurately.

By capitalizing on her good feelings and her positive abilities, Jean more than compensated for her mental and physical handicaps. Although working with her was tedious and frustrating for me at times, I enjoyed her enthusiasm and determination. I marveled at her high ability to concentrate on sounds and become completely wrapped up in her performing. She inspired me by her high level of courage and self-discipline.

Perhaps some of the success which teachers enjoy with handicapped children results from their adherence to these directives: (1) Never label a child as handicapped. All people are handicapped in some way (consider all who wear glasses). (2) Understand that the child is a person with deep feelings and unique potential. (3) Neither pamper him or dominate him. Show him his powers and get him to compensate for his weaknesses. (4) Show the child his contribution. He helps his teacher with his unique powers.

One aspect of music education needing improvement is the attitude that music activities for the handicapped should recreate and socialize these people. The actual truth is that some handicapped persons are less distracted by worldly preoccupations and can concentrate on serious music better than normal people. At least, it is safe to say that difficult and serious music is possible with many more handicapped children and adults than most teachers believe.[7]

Pupil productivity is sometimes low because teacher expectations are low.

A music teacher can be very helpful to a disabled child. Music has basic procedures which allow children who are otherwise limited to find new interests outside themselves and discover new respect and value in their own personhood because of their success and achievement. Music does more for these people in terms of their own feelings than in terms of actual musical achievements. For this reason performance-oriented educators, especially, experience much frustration when teaching the handicapped. The great contribution of music in the lives of the handicapped, then, is the releasing of their emotional forces since they are often unable to communicate or express themselves adequately in words or in academic study.

Teachers can often spot a disability which has not been previously noticed. Parents, easily embarrassed by deformity in their children, tend not to see deformities. Parents may, at times, not detect weaknesses because they have no way of comparing their child to others. The teacher of large classes may notice sluggishness in a child, but he sometimes only adds to the child's confusion by making the child less happy with himself. A music teacher who is able to meet this child alone or in small groups can readily notice an impairment in his ability to perceive, see, hear, or relate to the world about him. It is, of course, the duty of the teacher to notify the parents and discuss the child's welfare.

The Transfer Student

Many times the "emergency room" care for the transfer student requires more than first aid—it is quite an operation. Music teachers constantly complain of students who transfer to them. From teachers' comments, one concludes that transfer students universally have poor foundations. Transfer students cannot read simple music. (They may, however, bring difficult rote pieces which they like to play.) Transfer students cannot chord, improvise, transpose, or compose. They never seem to know how to practice and do not care about accuracy in notes, counting, or fingering. They hate music, have poor technique, have no sense of rhythm, and are unable to hear music in their minds.

What does all this say? It may say that teachers have blind love for their regular students. They enjoy teaching so much that they do not notice student needs or do not bother to provide a balanced program for their students. It may also indicate that teachers find it difficult to accept students who are still partially loyal to another teacher. Some teachers do not realize the integral role that rapport with students plays in their professional lives until they try to teach a student who has not developed rapport with them sufficiently because they are busy tearing down the rapport they had with a previous teacher.

The successful teacher gives the transfer student time to adjust. He realizes that the student must relinquish a certain jargon and phraseology as well as a method of attacking new material. Even when students transfer because of dissatisfaction with a previous teacher, there probably are many facets of the previous program to which they are still attached. Transfer students, then, need a teacher who shows respect for their past experiences and accomplishments.

Teachers can hinder student progress when they criticize a student's former teacher. The pupil usually feels adjusted to his previous teacher and his procedures. Hearing his former program criticized or ridiculed may threaten the student and somewhat paralyze his efforts. He cannot go back. He fears to go ahead. Successful teachers respect other professionals by maintaining a silence, at least, concerning conflicting pedagogical practices. They need to do this to foster the progress of the students who transfer to them.

> Where all think alike,
> No one thinks very much.
>
> Walter Lippmann

The Nonthinking Conformist

Many teachers like the conformist. They are never happier than when things are going according to routine. Some teachers think they are good and highly respected teachers when they are really in a rut. The cooperation of their students is an illusion. Human education requires interaction, interrelationships, and participation among human beings. Therefore, teachers can actually dehumanize students by robbing them of their dearest possession, their human responsibility. Teachers may think of themselves as "care-takin' folks," but in denying human rights to students they are taking away basic human privileges.

The nonthinking conformist, no matter how well he imitates his teacher, is *not* a good student. He has learned that his irresponsibility and lack of originality and personality win praises from a teacher who follows a method and a fixed sequence of procedures rigidly. Because of this, the student trains his fingers or his voice skillfully, but his personality is nonfunctioning.

Highly insecure students who are extremely hesitant in making decisions or using their own judgment often seek a teacher who expects a high degree of conformity. A teacher interested in a student's progress in attaining responsible maturity as well as heightened musical awareness, stimulates such a student with constant questions. Slowly he attempts to wean the student from his practice of thinking with other people's minds rather than his own.

Sibling Rivalry

Interfamily jealousy can be the source of discontent in music study. This is particularly true when students of unequal ability and age vie with each other for the loudest, fullest, and fastest sound.

The first way to cope with rivalry is to reduce conflict. To lessen the friction, the teacher may assign the rival students to different groups using contrasting approaches and materials. Little by little, students lose interest in comparing themselves with others.

Parents can create anxiety in children with their unrealistic expectations.[8] "Mary is the musician of our family," a parent may say, whereas her son Eric may have more depth and musical sensitivity than Mary. Here the teacher can be extremely helpful, by easing the parental pressure. He can discuss realistic goals with parents and students.

A third way to cope with interfamily rivalry is to accentuate the positve talents and abilities each child possess. Julie reads fast. Cathy has power. Julie has a keen mind. Cathy has more feeling and emotional meaning in her performance. To praise Julie's reading ability at Cathy's lesson may be a fatal mistake. However, it would be still worse to forget which abilities to build in Cathy at her lesson. By accentuating the positive, the teacher can reduce negative factors until they have little impact on students.

The Gifted

Johnny can read phenomenally fast, Susie has insights into interpretation that are most unusual, and Sam has flexibility and range that rank him as a genius. Although these students seem extremely gifted, their strengths are also accompanied by weaknesses. Johnny may be mechanical and have little imagination, Susie may tend to be inaccurate, and Sam may hate theory. Although the unusual talents these students have may seem overwhelming to a teacher, it is important to remember that weaker areas need reinforcement if the student is to mature fully. Because gifted people are often precocious, they need firm teachers. They need stabilizers to insist that they develop broadly as musicians. They also need firm rules for practicing and comprehensive programs including sight reading, theory, form, and analysis.

A gifted person needs a balanced attitude toward himself as well as a healthy attitude about music. He dare not rank himself as better than others. He needs objective praise which deals with the actual musical situation at hand. He needs to know that he is free to speak the language of music through his expressive playing, improvising, and composing. In other words, the gifted or highly talented student needs the freedom to be his best self. He needs enough conformity and dependency to stabilize him. He needs to know that no matter how excellent his performance becomes, he does not threaten his teacher.

Teachers often secretly fear gifted students. "What if he shows me up?" they ask themselves. They can dispel some of this fear if they realize that a gifted student is not usually as dependent on a teacher as a normal pupil. Although teachers need to stimulate and motivate the gifted to ensure progress, such students can learn facts for themselves. An instructor shows the talented how to read and where to find more information; they can educate themselves to a great extent.

Yet highly gifted students, because of years of unchallenging and boring tasks in school, may be lethargic. Early in childhood such wonder children behave precociously but, because they experience the sting of being called "misbehaving," often end up not trying to do anything. Not knowing how to learn as normal children, many gifted children withdraw and become socially maladjusted, their talents unused, perhaps unknown.

Because of the severe conflict in such gifted students between their superior powers and their roles as nonproducers, they are often nervous and emotionally overstimulated. They need a stable teacher who is not afraid of them. Often an average person is the best teacher for the gifted. Openmindedness and emotional stability are prime prerequisites in a teacher if students are to achieve personal growth and adjustment as well as musical prowess.

> If we take people as they are, we make them worse. If we treat them as if they were what they ought to be, we help them to become what they are capable of becoming.
>
> Goethe

The Emotionally Disturbed

Nervous twitches, squinting, jerking, or other persistent body mannerisms can be special danger signs in a youngster. Facial tics may have deep emotional roots.[9] Youngsters who show such symptoms betray the fact that emotional conflicts cannot be contained inside them anymore.

When a student exhibits deep emotional disturbance, however, the teacher encourages him to obtain professional help to diagnose and treat his problem.[10] Until the doctor comes to the rescue, the teacher continues to befriend the student and tries to relax him. By allowing the young person to talk freely, he is inviting the student to tell of his negative feelings of anger, jealousy, or rejection. Although the teacher is not a trained therapist and cannot analyze the student, his openness and empathy assuage the heat of the emotional battle within the student. Indeed, with his kindness and concern, the teacher may begin the healing process.

> Good discipline is a series of little victories in which a teacher, through small decencies, reaches a child's heart.[11]

The Misbehaving Student

A misbehaving pupil is using violent means to fulfill needs which have been neglected. Because he is subconsciously driven by an instinct to take care of himself, he does not always know why he acts mischievously or rudely. He does not necessarily dislike the people he hurts. He is restless and dissatisfied. He needs a teacher with a great deal of insight, a rich reservoir of caring concern, and a very high tolerance for stress.

Some students do naughty things because they crave the punishment they incur for misbehaving. Psychologists call such people "masochistic" because they seem to derive pleasure from being abused. Such a student will do anything to get his teacher angry enough to punish him. Therefore, the best way to treat a masochistic student is to ignore him in public and say quietly, "I'll see you after class." The student usually ceases such conduct if he knows it does not produce the desired effect.

Hostility toward the teacher can prompt a student to ruin a class. For centuries students have known that there is one way to hurt a teacher: prevent him from teaching. Sometimes when a student is disturbing the class, the teacher can examine what may be the cause of this hostility. Perhaps the teacher has slighted the student. What seems to be a very small matter to the teacher can be inflated in the student's mind to mean wholesale rejection. With sensitive awareness, a teacher can detect and remedy the situation before a student's anger grows.

A successful teacher tries to be objective and laconic during open conflict in the classroom. He comments on the public action and asks the student to see him later in the day. Alone with the student, the teacher makes him feel safe and at ease before discussing the conflict. The teacher, however, is careful not to speak to the student until he, too, has mastered his unruly feelings.

If, on the contrary, the teacher becomes outrageously angry during class because of misconduct, he can become the laughingstock of the class. Students have endless fun with "inflammable" teachers who show character weakness and a lack of emotional stability by losing their tempers easily. Infuriating a teacher is a favorite sport of students who feel a certain sense of power when they are able to produce a reaction in a teacher. To some extent, students have that feeling of control over a teacher even when the teacher merely reacts with mild feelings such as disgust or displeasure.

One day in May, Shelly, ten, sighed and said in a complaining tone, "How many more lessons do we have to take?"

I was annoyed by this and was about to make some corrective remark when I caught myself reacting adversely. I turned to her and said gently, "Shelly, you just said that to make me mad, didn't you?"

"Yeah, I guess so," admitted Shelly, a bit ashamed.

"Do you like to see me get mad?" I asked quietly.

"Yeah. I mean . . . well, you look so . . . well, anyway, I like to see you happy, too!'' Shelly confessed, trying to get herself out of a tight spot.

Very often a student misplaces his hostility for all authority and tries to punish the teacher since he cannot strike back at his parents, principal, or pastor. Such a student displays a very noticeable negative disposition and uses any person or thing to "kick at." His longing for supremacy and power is not merely that of a normal youth. His hostility causes him to want to dominate and punish others in revenge for the hurts he feels inside.

How does a teacher help such a student? First, it is important not to be surprised or allow oneself to feel personally attacked by the misplaced hostility. It is wise to accept the student as a trapped person who has unmet needs. His first need is to know that someone is concerned for him; then he needs to ventilate his feelings in a socially acceptable way. He could do this with physical movement as well as with minor leadership duties. He needs to know that he can be constructive, effective, and successful in using his power to help others. Above all, it is important to remember that the curative effect of dealing with such children does not necessarily seem successful at the time. Sometimes it takes years for a hostile student to find the deep meaning of his behavior and restore balance in his life. However, any kind concern he has met in any experiences along the way makes the unfortunate student richer.

Some "vandals" do not feel hostility or revenge but simply want to destroy in order to show power. They resent the lack of opportunity to do things constructively. They feel slighted when teachers do not allow them power to build programs or form class goals. Because they feel alone with nothing to call their own, they find it necessary to do such things as engraving their names in desks and ruining musical instruments or scores.

Misbehaving students are often low achievers. A teacher who is in contact with the level of competence of the student and watches to see that he feels successful, does not encounter behavior problems as often as other teachers. "A child who is succeeding in his work is rarely disruptive."[12]

Bored students misbehave. Many students suffer while their

teachers locate music during class, help individuals with private problems, and waste large amounts of time talking. Students also feel bored when music is too easy, when they feel that they are losing time, and when the music is not within their framework of interest. Because they feel that teachers do not care enough to teach them intelligently, students try to express their apathy and disgust by having a little forbidden fun.

Although a teacher must ask the group as a whole to pause for a short time during class, he can try to prevent boredom. He can engage the class's attention by asking all of them to be temporary teachers to the student who needs extra help immediately. "Say, class, what do you think, is he sharp or flat?" a teacher might ask a restless band. "Do you think Lisa is using diaphragmatic breathing?" the vocal teacher could ask the class when he perceives their need for a stimulating question.

No teacher suffers from serious discipline problems if he develops a warm, accepting relationship with each student. He keeps such problems out of his classes by watching closely how students are succeeding and reacting. Because he anticipates problems and prevents their development, the atmosphere of his classroom is positive and productive.

> Plenty of people in the profession are in no way worthy of the title of teacher. Historically in our culture, teaching has more often been a job than a profession.[13]

Self-Defeating Patterns of Relating

Irate, punitive words often do more harm than good. "Do that once more and I'll . . ." is a threat which may intensify angers in a student, may destroy the atmosphere of learning, may in fact invite the student to misbehave. To bribe a student with a reward is self-defeating, too, because it obligates a teacher to more and more bribes while they produce fewer and fewer results. Rewards are better than bribes because they come as surprises. Promising, however, is self-defeating in that it infers a lack of trust in the normal transactions between student and teacher. Continuous promising creates the attitude that nothing should be done unless a reward is promised. It can destroy mutual trust if it is used too much.[14]

Sharp, cutting sarcasm is also a two-edged sword which injures the teacher and the student. "Are you deaf?" "Were you born in a jungle?" "Are you that stupid?" are wounding questions that invite counterattacks which often injure a teacher's reputation after school hours.

Equally self-defeating is the giving of paradoxical messages. A teacher loses face when he brusquely asks for courtesy, when he noisily preaches the virtues of silence, and when he rudely commands politeness. Nonverbal behavioral messages prevail at such times; and a teacher reveals what he really feels, not what he is trying to cover up by his words.

Self-defeating patterns of coping with stress and conflict are not only ineffective; they are damaging. They may do irreparable harm by destroying students' positive self-image and will to learn. On the contrary, the use of positive means to build up students' self-image wins for teachers and students success in learning and the satisfaction of good human relationships.

Notes

1. Howard Lane and Mary Beauchamp, *Human Relations in Teaching* (New York: Prentice-Hall, 1955), p. 18.

2. Kathryn Bloom, "Development of Arts and Humanities Programs," *Toward an Aesthetic Education* (Washington, D.C.: Music Educators National Conference, 1971), p. 89.

3. David A. Thatcher, *Teaching, Loving and Self-Directed Learning,* p. 70.

4. Donald H. Clark and Asya L. Kadis, *Humanistic Teaching,* p. 85.

5. Frederick Perls, *In and Out the Garbage Pail,* p. 117.

6. Leonard Bernstein, "The Unanswered Question" (Norton lecture broadcast on radio station KSJR, July 1975).

7. Betty Welsbacher, "Music With Meaning: Special Education," *Gopher Music Notes* XXVIII (April 1972), 7.

8. Paul Henry Mussen and others, *Child Development and Personality,* p. 507.

9. Donald H. Clark and Asya L. Kadis, *Humanistic Teaching,* p. 148.

10. For a detailed description of how to decide on the need for help, types of help available, where to obtain it, how much to pay, and other questions, consult: Daniel N. Weiner, *A Practical Guide to Psychotherapy* (New York: Harper and Row, 1969).

11. Haim G. Ginott, *Between Teacher and Child,* p. 148.

12. Muriel Schoenbrun Karlin and Regina Berger, *Discipline and the Disruptive Child: A Practical Guide for Elementary Teachers* (West Nyack, N.Y.: Parker Publishing Co., 1971), p. 61.

13. Donald H. Clark and Asya L. Kadis, *Humanistic Teaching,* p. 27.

14. Haim G. Ginott, *Between Parent and Child,* pp. 31-49.

6

Raising Self-Concept in Students

> It was as if personality itself had a "face." This non-physical "face of personality" seemed to be the real key to personality change.[1]

What Is Self-Concept?

A student's self-concept is his mental picture of himself, a limiting blueprint of his personality which controls his choices in every area of his life. Although students, especially teenagers, are constantly asking themselves, "Who am I? What can I do? How high dare I aim?" they already possess a self-concept gained through countless childhood experiences.

A student's self-concept or self-image is the "I" or "me" within him which comprises the total meaning, goal-direction, and value tendencies he has as a person. This concept began developing when, as a baby, he had his first interaction with the environment. He then carefully measured his power or impotency in dealing with others and, in drawing conclusions, formed an image of himself. Now that he is older, he becomes ever more aware of himself and broadens his self-concept to include more complete interpretations. Conditioning from adults, identifications with others, and imitations of them, as well as countless personal choices, all work together to create a constant modification of a student's self-image.[2]

Dr. Maxwell Maltz, the plastic surgeon, was one of the first to become aware of the importance of self-image. Although his plastic surgery was successful, many of his patients continued to think of themselves as scarred and impotent people. After he attempted to change his patients' inner image of themselves and helped them to see themselves as successful, worthy persons, then and only then did the plastic surgery have its full effect in making the patients happy. Maltz watched his patients change their behavior patterns and begin new, successful lives. He and others have discovered that a person's self-image, formed in childhood and early youth, is relatively permanent. However, with the help of others and with deliberate energy, a person can remake his idea of himself and change his outlook on life.

Maltz believes that a healthy self-image makes people happy with themselves. He also firmly believes that self-image is the greatest predictor of success, failure, or change in behavior.[3] Maltz's experience with nervous and depressed patients acquiring new zest and success in life mainly through self-image changes proves that great things are in store for a person who has a high regard for himself.

The message in all of this is simply that music educators can predict success for their students not only through intense drilling and rehearsing; they can more readily expect success for students if the latter believe strongly in themselves as potentially successful. Teachers somewhat resemble the man who said, "I did not give my sons riches; instead I made them strong men who could win their own fortunes."

The music teacher can contribute notably to his students' happiness both by improving their self-image and the possibility of musical success and by helping them grow into more fully functioning persons. The following chart diagrams the student's gradual progress toward mature autonomy. First the student develops a positive and realistic self-concept; he begins to respect himself in spite of his limitations. Then he becomes aware of the opportunities and forces around him. By taking a further step, by acquiring the ability to relate to others realistically and effectively, he gradually becomes relatively secure and autonomous.

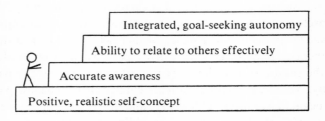

Integrated, goal-seeking autonomy

Ability to relate to others effectively

Accurate awareness

Positive, realistic self-concept

Causes for Bad Image

When Dr. Maltz altered the faces of people who had viewed themselves as ugly, distorted and scarred, he found that there was more to changing a person's disposition than beautifying his face. Emotional scars on a person's self-image are far more devastating than facial scars.

Where do these scars come from? They are the memories of hurts and rejections. Parents often reinforce a child's low self-esteem when they make such remarks as, "I know he can't do much—no one in our family is musical." This parent may think he is being humble and honest. However, his negative statement is highly unfair, since it lowers the level of aspiration in the child. At least, it can.

Society at large can cause a lowering of self-esteem. Society favors the rich, the capable, the popular, and the talented. When a child is inhibited and withdrawn, people are apt to say, "Yeah, Bruce—well, he ain't got much!" Unfortunately, Bruce hears that message, even if it is nonverbal, and he thinks of himself as worthless.

Frustrated teachers tend to reject their students when they do not seem to learn. Miss Nieken, for instance, snaps back at six-year-old

146

Grace who tries to answer a question. "You're wrong! Is that the best you can do?" she exclaims. Little Grace ponders over such acts of rejection for days and lowers her image of herself.

Ambitious teachers can also contribute to the lowering of esteem in students by expecting too much of them. Unrealistic demands place the student in a position of constant failure and struggle. Naturally, the student begins to belittle his powers of achieving.

Positive Self-Concept

Many students need positive thinking and a deepening of belief in themselves. They feel like cripples beside the strong; they feel small beside the large; they fumble and fail beside the teacher who succeeds with ease. Students must learn to believe in themselves and love themselves before they can run the race and win. Those who set out to compete with others must first build a positive position with regard to their own selfworth. Then only are they free and independent of the opinions of others. Persons having high esteem for themselves are not *highly* dependent on selfish ego-satisfactions, material things, or the applause of other people. They experience a wholeness, an integrity; and to some extent they can relax in that experience. Students who transcend others in self-acceptance are usually better equipped attitudinally to create or perform music in a truly aesthetic and personally involved way.

When a student has a positive self-concept, he accepts himself and is proud of his thoughts and feelings, whatever they are. He is emotionally honest and unashamed. For the most part, he does not need defensiveness, masks, or roles to excuse or hide his behavior.

How does this self-concept work in education? The most remarkable example of the power of positive self-concept I have ever encountered is that of Jane, a retarded child in a South Dakota school. The teacher told us that Jane had an IQ of 40; but, though she was rated as uneducable, she read beautifully. Upon our request, Jane brought her book over and read clearly, fluently, and accurately.

"How can this be?" we asked in amazement.

147

"I don't know!" responded the teacher. "I guess it is just that we never told Jane she couldn't read. Since she believed she could, she learned to read!"

Likewise, the concept a student has of himself determines largely what he will become. The belief that he is an important, worthwhile, uniquely talented (as well as limited) human being is the secret source of power within a successful person. Once a student lays hold of these facts about himself and constantly thinks positively—and realistically—about himself, he begins to live a creative and fulfilled life.

Constructive Evaluation

There are many ways to develop positive thinking and help students build a positive self-image. One such way is by constructive evaluation of their work. Teachers can be helpful in this way if they are objective in speaking of the here-and-now aspects of the situation: "You played. . . . Your next step. . . ." Teachers know when students play clearly and correctly. They know, too, when progress is praiseworthy. This is really all they can evaluate accurately.

However, imagine the teacher who, instead of being specific and precise in praising student work, says, "Jennie, you are magnificent! You are tremendous! What would I ever do without you?" This overpraise of personality would threaten Jennie. Because she would feel a bit wobbly from this unrealistic appraisal, her next efforts would probably result in "flubs" because she would want subconscious relief from these transcending labels on her personality. Teachers, on the other hand, who refrain from making sweeping generalizations, even positive ones, find that students improve when they hear precise evaluation of what they are doing well.

I shall never forget Michelle, who was seven. It did not take long for me to conclude that, though she was intelligent, she had been raised in an overprotective setting and had a very low self-image, believing that her "mommy" had to do everything for her. She was to learn to play the xylophone. Her coordination was poor, and I had a hard time being patient with her. At first she played only a little while, then stopped. I walked over to her and encouraged her by saying, "Look, Michelle, *you* did it! *You* played it all by yourself! Do more!" She looked up at me with some distrust but docilely played a few more notes. When she was alone again, she experimented with her own ability. When I returned she cried, "Hey, teacher, I can do it! I can do it all by myself!" Her big brown eyes were brimming with surprise and amazement as she began to realize that she was not only "mommy's little doll," but a capable young person. Michelle was never the same after that experience.

Teachers who praise what is laudable and hesitate to criticize what they are not sure is wrong are positive supports to students. Teachers usually know good performance when they meet it. They can only guess, however, about the personality of the performer. They can cause hurt feelings in students by their blunt statements criticizing the student himself rather than his musical behavior. "You are so slow," "You are never going to . . . ," "You don't really care," "You can't . . . ," "You're too stubborn," are all rash, presumptive statements which can be extremely damaging to the student. When teachers resist the tendency to project blame on the student himself and begin to evaluate student work specifically and in line with definite musical criteria, their remarks become curative and growth-producing.

> A child's psychic personality is far different from our own, and it is different in kind and not simply in degree.[4]

Apt Analogies

A student feels positively about himself and his environment when his teacher uses apt analogies. To a college boy who is extremely hostile because he failed an examination, a statement like, "Sing as if you hated somebody," may help him release some disturbing emotions as well as help him feel accepted in spite of his feelings. To Joey, the little farm boy, an analogy likening the horsepower in his fingers to the horsepower in his daddy's tractor is appealing. To little Lisa, the mention of her doll makes music meaningful. Lisa feels good about herself when she thinks of her important role as mother to her dolls.

At times a teacher can liken the movement of a piece to some familiar rhythmic experience in a student's life. Greg, fifteen, for instance, was learning to play "Jesu, Joy of Man's Desiring," but his rhythmic impact was sluggish. To remedy this, I told him to picture a large baroque cathedral with its massive pillars and their spiraling decorations. I sang the tune and traced arcs in the air to give him the rhythmic feel. "Do you feel it better now, Greg?" I asked.

"Yeah, I guess so, but I think I know a better way to feel the beat," offered Greg, much to my amazement.

"Tell me about it," I said.

"Well, it feels to me like I'm riding a bike. You know, you put your foot on the bike pedal and go down, then round, down, then round," he said as he traced circles rhythmically in the air. To Greg's bicycle-oriented generation, this analogy made more sense than references to cathedrals.

When teachers use apt analogies, they not only educate by using clear and enthusiastic examples; they also elevate a student's positive regard for himself and his unique life-style. Such teachers show that they can put their subject, music, into the individual framework of the student's life by linking environment or experience with the elements of music. In this way, they make the students feel at ease and ready for learning. Not everything is strange.

Consider well what your strength is equal to and what exceeds your ability.

Horace

Realistic Self-Concept

Being honest about a student's limitations and needs is self-image seen from its realistic aspect. A concert career is a realistic goal for very few students. Musicians are sad and frustrated more because of their unrealistic self-concept than because of any other factor. If a teacher is realistic, he attempts to find the student's actual dimensions of power and weakness. Just how talented, how ambitious, and how persistent is this student? What are his limitations, needs, and personal drives? Until he knows these things, a teacher cannot make serious plans for a student's musical education.

> Not all children can or should become accomplished artists; all children can and should develop aesthetic sensibility. . . . There should be a constant interflow . . . among all subjects and activities, to prevent false distinctions between work and play, the arts and the sciences, thought and feeling.[5]

Am I Talented?

Every student asks himself: "Am I talented? Should I study music?" Because he sees others perform with facility and ease, he wonders if he should continue to try. Unfortunately, teachers often fail to define musical talent sufficiently to put their students at ease. However, even psychologists do not agree on an exact definition. Carl Seashore defined a musically talented person as one who could perceive loudness, pitch, time, and timbre to a superior degree.[6] Mainwaring, the English psychologist, called musical talent a linguistic ability. He likened a musical person to one who could perceive loudness, pitch, time, and timbre to a

Since no psychologist has adequately defined talent, the quest for a simple definition is fruitless. Of central interest here is the fact that a teacher in rapport with his students is "in tune" with the area of talent in which each of his students excels. It is commonly accepted that talent is complex. Each person has his own individual assortment of weak and strong powers, of interests and delights in musical experiences. In actual performance a person uses three organs or senses to perceive music: the eye (reading, gauging intervals), the ear (pitch, loudness, timbre), and the hand or foot (rhythm, instrumental technical management). Usually a student has outstanding talent in some areas and less in others. One student has perfect pitch but lacks muscle strength and precision or rhythmic steadiness. Another has a rare ability to read but has poor taste in dynamics or does not have keen sensitivity in music appreciation.

Further, students are fascinated by different aspects of music. Teachers who are alert to these forces within students can guide them more effectively. For example, some students are interested in percussion, and they are excited by brilliant, quick-moving sound. One student excels in coordination and another in artistic sensitivity, while a third, with his lively creative imagination, has a burning interest in building a new sound and a new era in music. Any teacher who is too dull and regimented to want to study and explore the multifaceted talent structure within his students will lose many opportunities to realize human potentialities. The world is worse for such neglect.

A certain amount of musical talent is an inborn or innate sensitivity to sound. Rosina Lhevinne of the Julliard School of Music once said, "Talent to me means a special inner creative ability. . . . A genuine love for music and the determination to work hard to achieve one's goals also imply talent."[8]

Since "talent" is a nebulous and relatively unmeasurable factor, it is realistic not to stress the need of having it. Talent is a tool; it enables a person to perceive, perform, or create music with relative ease. Any tool is useful when it is used. It is the primary task of the music educator to stimulate the use of this tool, talent.

Suzuki, after his vast sampling and success with Japanese children, writes that anyone who can learn to speak his native tongue has musical talent.[9] He writes: "Talent is common, but a favorable environment is not. . . . All human beings are born with great potentialities. We must investigate methods."[10] Although the Suzuki approach is somewhat at odds with the humanistic approach of this book, the idea of the universality of talent is common to both systems. William James, the American psychologist, was one of the first to see that talent is not only very common but that a vast amount of potential within each person is being wasted. He estimated that most people use only 10 percent of their potential and that they can "alter their lives by altering their minds."[11]

> There is something that is much more scarce,
> something finer far; something rarer than ability.
> It is the ability to recognize ability.
>
> E. Hubbard

Personal Drive

Partly because talent is undefinable and intangible, it becomes a handy cop-out for teachers and students. The frustrations of poor performing and poor reading so disgust and anger teachers that they project the blame entirely on lack of talent. They find themselves saying, "If the teenagers were talented, they would . . . ," "If only my choir were talented and perceptive enough to . . . ," "If Sally were talented, she would practice."

Does talent include with it a personal drive? Do talented people have a special reinforcing compulsion to achieve musical skills? Obviously not. Some of the most gifted musicians lack other qualities that are needed to develop their talent. On the other hand, there is no successful musician who does not have some talent and very much drive and persistence. The ambition to want to develop one's innate abilities and the determination to advance gradually but steadily toward excellence and artistry are most necessary for student musicians.

Before planning a music career with a student, it is advisable to check annually the qualities of talent, ambition, and persistence or perseverance of the student as well as his other interests and financial backing. By being levelheaded at the start, teachers can prevent ruined careers.

I'm happy when I get a song I know I can play
and still learn from it. When I see a song I know I
can play I get ambitious. When I get disgusted
you can bet it has something to do with hard
music. I get eager when I get a song that's fun to
play.

Allen Selinski, 12

Practice

Students who understand their own limitations can direct their
attention toward reasonable goals during practice. A realistic self-
image and realistic goal setting allow the student to be comfortable
and positive as he works toward a short-term, very possible goal.
Encouraged by attaining each small goal, the student goes on to
work for a slightly higher goal. When a student, on the other hand,
is overambitious and strives to attain unreasonable goals or to
reach possible goals but in an unreasonably short time, he is nervous, frustrated, and anxious. A pianist's fingers may freeze from
fear of not reaching a goal, and a singer's throat may tighten as he
tries to do things which are unrealistic for him at his stage of artistry.

The teacher who is truly in touch with limits and potentialities of
the student helps the student to be realistic in two areas: goal setting
and goal achieving. That is, he restrains the student from aiming
too high and aids the student in selecting the means of attaining the
skills he wants.

It is unrealistic, for instance, for a student with severe asthma to
aim at playing a flute. A student with poor coordination should be
encouraged not to compete with a highly talented, well-coordinated
friend. It is unreasonable for a teacher to take a mother seriously
when she announces proudly, "Leila is only fourteen now; but she
will be a music major. We are looking for the best conservatory we
can find." Such a statement is not only unrealistic but ludicrous
when, upon examination, Leila shows that she cannot read music
beyond the beginner's level.

However, when a child is persistent, he can work to overcome any obstacle. Dean, for instance, early in the third grade, was helped to believe that he could sing by Sister Adeline, his teacher, who told him he could learn like other people and acted on that belief. At the first report card conference Dean's father had said, "I can't sing. I can see why he can't. He'll never sing: he's just like the rest of us." Yet the father's voice had a beautiful inflection and a musical ring. Sister Adeline, not satisfied with this defeatist attitude, had gone up to Dean as the other children were singing and had sung into his ear. She had used hand gestures, desk tracing, and body positions as well as endless drill. By the spring of the year Dean was singing as well as his classmates. In fact, he had such confidence in himself that he wanted to lead the class.

Although progress in music is sure and rapid when students are motivated, there are many students who do not practice. They do not believe in themselves or do not feel the desirability of attaining musical skills or understandings. Sometimes these students feel a deep jealousy for, or antipathy toward, a successful student. For instance, a monotone may cling to the stance "I hate music," as a form of escape, a form of feeling rejected without looking rejected to his classmates.

These students are magnifying the negative aspects of practicing. When the fear, anxiety, or humiliation are taken out of music practice, on the other hand, a student can make concrete plans, issue realistic deadlines, and stay within the limits of his stress tolerance. Because he accepts his limits and inabilities, he is able to practice slowly without embarrassment. He can listen to himself on tape without becoming discouraged. He is realistic in seeing slight improvements and sets out courageously to make further gains.[12]

I have never seen a natural musician. Performing music, is, in many ways, a parallel activity to sports.[13]

Sometimes a teacher is vague in his promises that a student will acquire whatever skill he is trying to acquire. When the student does not have it in a week, he feels he must be stupid or untalented. Some teachers find it advisable to "level with the student" by telling him, friend to friend, that it will take six months of daily practice to get, for instance, diaphragmatic breathing. If he does not practice it except at lessons, it will necessarily take many years to develop. If he practices daily for a few months, he may have it soon. Putting the final goal a few calendar months away may remove the frustration of the student. However, for some students, six months is forever and the goal beyond the horizon. Dealing with such a student, the teacher sets preliminary goals such as: "It should only take a few weeks before you can breathe correctly in your vocal exercises."

Some gifted students do not practice much because they feel programmed to take it easy. For these, their high degree of talent is a natural invitation to laziness. A brilliant student who can meet ordinary competition without effort may learn to be idle. To obtain a higher level of achievement, he not only has to overcome his natural inertia; he must also conquer the temptation to ride along on his own talent. For this and other reasons, many talented students do not succeed in music.

Therefore, while talent is quite common, the capacity for hard work and good practicing is exceptional. The highly endowed are gifted with bodies that coordinate, ears that perceive, souls that speak poetically. However, the great virtuosos are not only gifted with talent; they also have the drive and the self-discipline that make them practice stubbornly and persevere in spite of failure and fatigue.

Because music is a highly complex art and each person has a unique composite of talents, skills, and ambitions, it is highly unfair to compare one student with another. Yet because this is so commonly done, there is much dissatisfaction in music departments. Joey excels in music listening; Brian has strong fingers; David plays with good interpretation—each is king in his own world. The teacher leads the student to accept himself in his strengths, to work hard to eliminate his weaknesses, and—above all—never to compare his progress with that of others. Such building up of ego strength in a student is as important as the engendering of a love for music. For this reason Rosina Lhevinne believed that the first teacher, not the last, is the most important for any student.[14]

An ambitious student with a realistic self-image will work hard and consider his effort more important than his innate talent. He believes in himself, believes in music, and finds a joy in creating beautiful sounds. Because he sees music as desirable, he opens the door to learning from within himself. By means of strong intrinsic motivation, he does not need to be nagged, coaxed, or bribed. He does not expect prizes or rewards in the form of grades or honors. He reaches out for music and attains what he strives for. Such a student looks with disgust on a teacher who offers rewards for attaining goals. Music, for him, is its own reward.

Let the child go at his own pace. Regardless of parental pressure, a child cannot go at anyone else's pace that is not appropriate for him. However, to recognize at the outset that a child does his own pacing is very important.[15]

Limits of Stress

Ambitious teachers can, at times, have unrealistic expectations for their students. Expectations can be realistic for one student and unrealistic for another because no two people are alike in their capacity for stress. Since factors such as physique, temperament, heritage, training, and life experiences differ in each individual's life, all people vary in their ability to tolerate stress.

Wise teachers watch students and observe evidence of fatigue, discouragement, and frustration. They also try to emphathize with them when they show signs of exhaustion, thus encouraging them to admit their feelings. After a certain stage of fatigue is reached, no student can gain profit from further practice. He will, perhaps, become negative about the music program or even question the desirability of music study itself.

Privacy

Because learning involves personal change and each student reaches out by his own learning style to acquire educational gains, he needs a certain amount of privacy. Wise teachers deeply respect this privacy. They know that a student feels violated when an unwanted person intrudes upon his personal life, especially upon his inner space of intimacy.

The various influences of his environment must jell within each student. After a teacher tells him about specific behavior, skill, and attitudinal changes, a student feels the need to retreat into the quiet room of his mind to appraise himself and build his self-image. When a teacher oversteps the rules of privacy and tries to impose self-image attitudes, the student feels uncomfortable. A student needs proofs of his self-worth. But he is the one to put them together and arrive at an "aha" experience of discovery. He needs privacy to build himself into the person he wants to become. An invasion of privacy angers a student and can stunt his growth. Usually a student does not know quite why it is that his teacher revolts him. Unable to explain himself or help clear up the problem, he responds in apathy and loses interest in his music study.

Relating through Sensitive Awareness

People who mistrust themselves and harbor feelings of inferiority, fear, and hostility constantly misinterpret situations and make false assumptions about what others mean by their actions and words. In other words, they have an inaccurate awareness of the world around them. Because of the spirit of competition within music departments, music students can become suspicious and jealous. They worry that others are trying to surpass them. Because students can have a distorted view of what is going on around them and because success means so very much to them, they may experience problems in relating to others.

When students have warm, positive, honest feelings about themselves, people around them do not threaten them. Because they believe they are valuable and worthy people, they dare approach professors and peers to speak freely and to assess a situation without distortion.

Relationships depend on trust. If a person is suspicious about how another may be cheating or trapping him, he cannot relate comfortably to that person. An assertive person who detects some trickery will openly confront the suspected person. The person who is a bit paranoid has inaccurate awareness and fears that such an investigation would be too painful for him. Hence, he prefers to live with poor relating ability.

Success Mechanism

Deep in the subconscious of every person is a system which he can use effectively to heighten his success in music. Most authors do not know exactly how this "goal-directing mechanism"[16] works. Dr. Maltz believes that there is in the subconscious of every person a system which is not a mind, but something like an inner machine made up of the brain and nervous system. This power, which is directed by the human mind, works quite automatically. When a person sets it for success, it produces success. Carl Rogers calls this phenomenon a "spontaneous force within the organism which has the capacity of integration and redirection."[17] Therefore, the man who consistently programs himself mentally for success, usually achieves it. However, an individual's emotions can interfere and seriously set the nonthinking apparatus off course. If a person shifts from his mind-set and allows his feelings to replace his intellect as goalsetter, he can veer off course and begin to fail.

Examples of how the goal-directing mechanism brings success could fill many books. Some outstanding athletic heroes are examples of this phenomenon. The slow-footed boy whom the coach called "Rocket" in laughing ridicule determined to take up the challenge and did win fame as a world-famous runner. Another athlete, a weak boy who was once called "Muscles," became a famous fighter. These men turned criticism into goals and geared their inner mechanisms to success.

Likewise, musicians set their goals and achieve them. A conductor can raise his baton in precisely the right position. His players know where he is in the dynamic scale and just where to stress their notes in response to his goal-directing mechanism. The entire nonverbal behavior of the conductor speaks for the subconscious goal-directing mechanism which he has deep inside.

Space does not permit a discussion of the mystery of the workings of the mind and the goal-setting and goal-achieving activities of a determined individual. No psychologist, theologian, philosopher, or doctor really understands the marvelous workings of the most complex of all creations, the human mind. Suffice it to say that positive thinking and realistic goal setting sets an individual up for success.

The positive determination to succeed integrates a person and because it unites his entire mental and physical forces, it brings as much success as is realistic for that person. The use of this drive toward success is necessary for both the genius and the moderately talented. Because some seemingly talented students are aimless and goalless, they achieve little. On the other hand, because of a fixed resolution coupled with indefatigable courage and diligence, the average student can develop a high degree of musical skill.

> Not find a barkeep unto Jove in me?
> I have remained resentful to this day
> When any but myself presumed to say
> That there was anything I couldn't be.
>
> Robert Frost[18]

The Role of the Imagination

Often a student idolizes a famous performer and sets his goal to be able to imitate the sound and style of that person. How many little cornetists have worked assiduously for hours trying to become like Al Hirt? It is not unusual for a child to sit for hours blowing sour notes on his horn and experiencing much pleasure because, in his imagination, he hears the sound of a great trumpeter coming from his horn. He feels famous and powerful.

Students gain new enthusiasm, too, when, they imagine a mood or a story and play or sing in that spirit. Instrumentalists and singers can "tell stories" in sound even at an early age. Adele Marcus, pianist and teacher, believes that every teacher must make a choice as to whether he wants the student to be a "finger pusher" or a creative musician.[19]

The imagination plays a great part in the singing of large skips and the moving of hands for long leaps. The artist learns to imagine or expect a certain pitch and his muscles automatically fix themselves for that sound. After the tone is set deep in the performer's subconscious, it can be produced easily even when his nervousness tips him off balance.

Further, the imagination can help clarify music in a person's mind and greatly reduce the need for practice. The pianist Alfred Schnabel took lessons for only seven years. He hated practice but loved music. He memorized music away from the keyboard, played in his imagination, and then went to the keyboard and played as if he had practiced long hours. He knew of the power of his imagination as well as the idea that a human being usually acts and feels about himself as he imagines himself to be.

The powers of his self-image bring a person into new contact with his best, positive self. Negative feelings become less disturbing as one begins to find that he is not "pushed around" by emotional upheavals since he sees things in a realistic perspective. Constant searching effort must continue for a man to keep constantly discovering his true self. John Charles Thomas, for instance, was a man who loved life and had a great deal of self-confidence. Before every concert he looked into the mirror and told himself, "I will sing well tonight." And he did.

> Don't figger how you can't.
> Figger how you can.
>> Daniels
>> (Tennessee Philosopher)

A positive self-image is the best companion a student can take with himself to a contest. The secret of positive assurance and goal-directed thinking is that it often turns the "as if" thought of the prospective winner to the "it is!" happiness of the actual winner.

When the self-image is intact and secure, the contestant feels "good." When it is threatened, he is anxious and apprehensive. Though a certain degree of excitement is inevitable in such circumstances, a positive-minded student is free from negative hang-ups and feels free to be himself. He is not ashamed of himself or his music; in fact, he is proud to express himself musically. There is no screen of distraction keeping him from the music. The music is not "out there"; instead, his creative expression and deepest soul are one with the music, which comes to life through his performance or conducting.

It is of utmost importance that a person prepare well for contests. The goal-directed person makes the rules of the contest his serious guide. A positive thinker need not be a dreamer or a fool. He meticulously measures his precision, balance, quality, and finesse. When these factors are constant goals throughout preparation, success is inevitable.

Concert artists who have felt the stress of competitions realize that these events are regrettably painful; yet they see no other way that will so effectively bring the truly powerful person to show his ability and autonomy as a performer. The spring contest system has served the public schools effectively for over fifty years.[20]

If and when there is a shift in the emphasis of music in the public school system from performance to human development in music, contests may lose some of their attractive force. The festival idea, which would be more in line with the humanistic approach, would stimulate music study. Students need goals to work for. However, goals which stimulate instrinsic motivation are preferable to those which encourage students to work for extramusical rewards.

> You can read a child's image of himself in.his actions. If he thinks he's tough it shows. . . . We act like the person we think we really are.[21]

When a student possesses high self-esteem and feels supported by a reinforcing teacher, he succeeds in areas where less positive students fail.

When a student experiences the warm acceptance of his teacher, he is more capable of concentrating on demanding activities such as sight reading. Because he sets his goal on reading accurately the first time through, his whole person is integrated. His energies are directed toward comprehending the tricky rhythms and complex notation on the page.

Because negative thoughts are greatly reduced by his high self-esteem, his rapport with his teacher, and an accepting educational climate, the student is free to succeed in his efforts to sight-read.

Likewise, when a student enjoys the security of a freeing climate, he may find more success in performing "by ear." Liberated from the freezing influence of self-consciousness, the performer is able to develop tonal imagery. He can memorize motives, sequences, and repetitions of both melodic and rhythmic materials. Tonal imagery, which is the hearing of sounds before singing or playing them, is a vital force in all musical activity. "By ear" performing reinforces a student's memorization and his analysis of a piece for its intervalic relationship as well as the motion of the melody and harmony.

A staunch belief in self and the security of a good relationship with one's teacher form a good beginning for the memorization of music. Since the prime prerequisite for memorization is the removal of fears and anxieties, a secure student programs himself for a music-conscious, rather than a mistake-conscious, performance.

The positive emotions of cognitive self-assertiveness come into full play as a performer reaches out to lay hold and reconstruct a piece of music within his mind and psycho-motor system. Since fear is the antithesis of thought[22] and forms, to some extent, a closing of the mind to reality, the fearful person experiences a feeling of helplessness. He finds himself facing a twofold battle. He must handle his negative emotions and remember and organize his musical material. In order to accomplish this feat, a performer must develop a healthy egoism, a positive self-image, and direct his goal-setting mechanism toward success.

Current literature features many memory strategies. Bower, for instance, suggests that a student reshuffle his "cognitive priorities."[23] He must steady his gaze exactly on what he wants to remember. He may not go on until he has fully absorbed that material. Eye, ear, and muscle sensations must be programmed precisely. Then he must associate this with former learning. In other words, the student really puts the new material within his cognitive field, placing it meaningfully in comparison or contrast with other learnings.

Although each teacher usually has his own favorite methods of memorizing, most techniques hinge on one threefold principle: involvement, concentration, and deliberation. When a student takes his time and really lives his music fully in his mind, he can more easily relive that music again. When he brings his senses into full function—his eyes seeing clearly; his ears hearing fully so as to be able to predict the sound the next time; his hands feeling the spatial relationships and adjustments, and his mind analyzing, naming, and comparing the phrases—there is hope that this student will remember his music when asked to play from memory.

The personal involvement of the student forestalls failure. To the student who is convinced of his self-worth and his success in music study, music is not a frill which he can throw off when he becomes too busy in other subjects. If he learns in a freeing atmosphere created by a humane teacher, if he becomes so involved that he enjoys "peak experiences" at times, music is more than a frantic scramble for notes.

> May we never again tell a child not to sing, just to move his lips! Hundreds of thousands of adults are obediently doing just that.[24]

164

Notes

1. Maxwell Maltz, *Psycho-Cybernetics* (New York: Essandess Special Editions, 1968), p. vii.

2. Robert J. Klausmeier and Richard E. Ripple, *Learning and Human Abilities,* p. 560.

3. Maxwell Maltz, *Psycho-Cybernetics,* p. ix.

4. Maria Montessori, *The Secret of Childhood,* p. 69.

5. Charles E. Silberman, *The Open Classroom Reader* (New York: Random House, 1973), p. 749.

6. Carl Seashore, *Psychology of Music* (New York: McGraw-Hill Book Co., 1938), pp. 2-3.

7. J. Mainwaring, "The Meaning of Musicianship: A Problem in the Teaching of Music," *British Journal of Educational Psychology* XI (1941), 205-214.

8. Quoted by James Bastien, *How To Teach Piano Successfully* (Park Ridge, Ill.: General Words and Music Co., 1973), p. 398.

9. Van Sickle, "Suzuki Principles Not New," *Gopher Music Notes* XXVI (December 1969), 5.

10. Shin'ichi Suzuki, *Nurtured By Love,* p. 109.

11. Frank Goble, *The Third Force,* p. 56.

12. Leopold LaFosse, "Teaching the Art of Practicing," *The Instrumentalist* XXVIII (December 1973), 42-43.

13. Henry Mancini, "Discover Music through Popular Music," The *Instrumentalist* XXVII (September 1973), 32-33.

14. Quoted by James Bastien, *How to Teach Piano Successfully,* p. 398.

15. Daniel N. Weiner and E. Lakin Phillips, *Training in Self-Discipline and Self-Control* (Englewood Cliffs, N.J.: Prentice-Hall, 1971), p. 115.

16. Maxwell Maltz, *Psycho-Cybernetics,* p. 14.

17. Carl Rogers as quoted by Roberto Zavalloni, *Self-Determination* (Chicago: Forum Books, 1962), p. xi.

18. Robert Frost, "Auspex," in *In the Clearing* (New York: Holt, Rinehart and Winston, 1962), p. 59.

19. Adele Marcus, "Creative Study and Practicing," *Clavier* VIII (January 1969), 38-39.

20. Emil Holz, "The Very First National School Band Contest," *The Instrumentalist* XXVII (June 1973), 34-36.

21. Mack R. Douglas, *How to Make a Habit of Succeeding* (Grand Rapids, Mich.: Zondervan Corp., 1966), p. 161.

22. Nathaniel Branden, *Breaking Free* (Los Angeles: Nash Publishing Corp., 1970), p. 140.

23. Gordon H. Bower, "How to . . . uh . . . Remember!" *Psychology Today* VII (October 1973), 63-70.

24. Virginia D. Austin, "Striking a Balance Between Participation and Perfection," *Music Educators Journal* 60 (March 1974), 35.

7
Success through Rapport

In which ways can rapport contribute to success in music education? How does a teacher go about assuring success and preventing failure through relational practices? First of all, a teacher must investigate the limits of his stress tolerance and his orientation towards teaching so he can truly and more consciously control his relating practices. He forms a definite style of role-behavior which promotes success, seeing himself as a facilitator of learning rather than as an authoritarian ruler. Finally, a successful person is one who aims high. He does not see music education as a form of physical education which develops digital and muscular skills. He sees it, rather, as an opportunity to help each of his students to grow into a whole person. He aims at facilitating the total involvement of the student through high-level involvement in music tasks.

Most teachers start out idealistic and well-intentioned but are gradually overcome by the powerful contingencies in their working environment. Underbudgeting, overcrowding and an administrative ethos that insists that you "go along to get along" guarantee frustration for teachers, a frustration likely to be displaced downward upon those who can least resist—the student.[1]

One of the greatest contributing factors to failure in music education is fatigue. When a teacher feels irritable and exhausted, he often becomes laissez-faire and either lowers his standards of performance or the quality of his relationship with his students. Teachers can remedy or, better, forestall teaching failures by learning to keep within their stress tolerance limits. Once a person knows what his energy level is, he does well to put a ceiling on his expectations of himself. He does better work if he cuts off any activities which go beyond his personal energy limits. However, many people overwork because they have difficulty assessing their level of energy. Human vitality remains a mystery. Why does a person fluctuate in his stress tolerance? What is the nature of human energy? How can one maintain and increase energy in oneself?

One effective method of maintaining energy is keeping oneself physically fit. A fit person possesses dynamic health because he has balance in his life. He feels the rhythm of life within him through physical exercise, work, relaxation, and good sleeping and eating habits. He possesses peace of mind because of a relatively stable set of values and a sensible approach to mental health.

Regular exercise contributes much to acquiring physical fitness. Each person can develop his own pattern, choosing anything from daily walking and setting-up exercises to cycling, long-distance running, or swimming. Research shows that fit teachers are more confident, positive, and optimistic. They can endure greater struggles in teaching because their nervous systems are "conditioned to function strongly and in good balance." Their bodies are alert and ready for work or for relaxation at any time.[2]

The anxieties of teaching make great demands on the human heart. Since fear and anxiety consist of an inner "freezing" and a tendency to cope with a situation internally rather than to engage in outgoing behavior, the blood vessels tend to constrict the blood. Dr. Cureton writes:

> In testing with sophisticated procedures . . . recording the activity of the heart nerves (pre-ejection intervals), we find out that many peo-

ple today are suffering from nervous tension as measured on these heart nerves, and this handicaps the body enormously in its vigor and its health. In sedentary life this heart tension grows.[3]

This heart tension grows and can kill a person if he is confronted with a sudden traumatic conflict. In an extremely emotional moment the profuse secretion of adrenalin in a person's body makes too great an impact on his heart and he dies. When a person is physically fit, on the contrary, the human heart can take the larger doses of adrenalin secreted at times of strong fear or anger. During strenous exercise the heart adjusts to stress and builds endurance and strength.[4] The heart and muscles of an exercising person become more sturdy, more vigorous, and more ready for enduring effort; and the psychological effect of regular and proper physical exercise is also quite impressive. Persons feel more fully alive, raise their self-image, and improve their attitudinal and inspirational levels.[5]

Calisthenics, running, or even the mild forms of Yoga make the body feel integrated and fully alive. The good feelings and sentiments within a person at such times are "positive and expansive" and cause a flow of "tonic and vitalizing hormones." According to Alain, a Yoga expert, the bad feelings a person has help the body produce "depressing and devitalizing toxic substances."[6] He believes that the mosquito, the bee, and the cobra inject their toxic secretions into their enemies. Only man poisons himself with his negative feelings and retains the consequent toxic hormones within his body. If this theory is true, it is a convincing argument for the teacher to keep himself physically fit.

Finally, recent studies comparing variances in pulse rate to levels of teacher-student interaction, show that more physically fit teachers rank higher in interpersonal relations.[7] A good physique provides the courage and strength needed to interact with people displaying indirect behaviors three and four listed by Ned Flanders in his Interaction Analysis System. The teacher relates better to his students, and the really fit person makes less of a demand on his cardiovascular system when teaching, thereby enhancing his stress tolerance. One factor leads to another:

Fitness ——→ Better Interaction ——→ Less Strain on Heart ——→ Greater Tolerance for Stress

Tolerance for Teaching Music

Some musicians, having received superior training in performance, may be keenly sensitive to error and have a low level of tolerance for teaching beginners or the very young. The artist who fails on the concert stage is often a poor candidate for teaching grade school music classes. The orientation of such a person is toward perfect performance as well as toward the art of music rather than toward the student. He is not usually attuned to the expectations and needs of beginners in music.[8]

Performer-teachers often have difficulty coping with music problems which are removed from their experience. The virtuoso may have forgotten his humble beginnings. He cannot empathize with the amateur's groping attempts, his pain-giving and constant errors, his musical preferences. Specialists in music have a tendency to become estranged from the human struggle to attain musical skills because of the ease and facility with which they perform. It is true that all performers struggle with music which is challenging to them. Specialists, however, see no struggle in elementary materials.

Even more important than physical fitness, and closely related to the musicians' fitness for teaching, is their personal tolerance for stress. Limitations in stress tolerance are produced by a wide range of causes, all fundamentally emotional. Teachers who succeed are in touch with their personal tolerance for stress. Like others, they feel the fatigue and pressures which family and teaching responsibilities bring to them, but they have the courage to admit that because of their values and personal priorities they are unable to meet some expectations of others.

The life-force within each person, strengthened by emotional power, is capable of phenomenal feats. However, due to lack of self-knowledge and introspection, music teachers can allow emotional forces within them to break down their tolerance. If a teacher's energy is spent largely in coping with inner anger, depression, and a feeling of being trapped, his stress tolerance in music class may become seriously lessened. After studying teachers' behavior, Bowers and Soar concluded:

> A teacher must care, must not have this concern blocked by her own intrapersonal tensions, and must be relatively free of distorting mechanisms and able to enter honestly into relationships with others. Perhaps what this reduces to is that a teacher must be able to use her "self" openly, clearly, and honestly in her interactions with pupils.[9]

To build stress tolerance, then, a teacher must face himself and admit his feelings, needs, and expectations. He also must know that sharing them with others lessens the impact of bottled up emotions and projects the energy into a common cause. Admitting a personal feeling ·to students in a sincere, nonthreatening way frees the students as well as the teacher. It also greatly heightens the tolerance for stress present in that particular situation.

Tolerance for Interpersonal Friction

Because their interpersonal relationships are not sufficiently established, some music educators feel distressed. During years of development young performers spend countless hours practicing alone while their peers are socializing. Because talented young people feel inspired to compete with others at the time in their lives that they should be learning to socialize, they may find themselves lacking in ability to relate. Further, as a student finds meaning and expression in musical performance, he feels some satisfaction in his need to communicate socially. Such a musician does not feel the need to develop verbal skills to as great an extent as do his non-musical friends.

However, when a teacher realizes that success in teaching depends largely upon relating to students and helping them develop their potentialities, he can change. He can shift from rigid, fixed ways and become flexible and adaptable. He can begin to notice and care for the student as a growing person, not only as a performer.

171

Stress tolerance limits will rise when a teacher becomes aware of the needs and feelings of his students. Only after an individual sensitizes himself to the emotional drives, frustrations, and goals of students can he guide the educational process in this direction. When he knows more of the "whole man" of his student, an educator can save himself from the anxiety caused by negative feelings about his success in music education.

Just accepting as fact that children and adolescents are thoughtless, uninhibited, and somewhat irresponsible, that they anger and threaten their teachers, releases some pressure. Also, in reading the feelings of students, a teacher remembers that he and they, in varying personal ways, share the pain, disappointment, failure, and limitation inherent in the human condition. With empathy and caring respect the teacher increases the tolerance for stress in himself, in his students, and in their interaction.

Teachers can also meet resistance from students and increase pressures on them by using an authoritarian type of leadership when students yearn for democratic procedures. Students crave a certain amount of acceptance and respect even though they realize that their teachers are, possibly, far more intellectual and gifted than they. They seek a bond of friendship with the teacher sufficient to maintain the courage to pursue their goals in spite of their, as yet, meager attainments in music skills and understanding.

> See yourself as a winner—
> Watch your relating improve!
>
> See your students as winners—
> Watch their performance improve!

Teaching Style Limitations

Because highly endowed teachers tend to have trouble knowing how to relate to others, they often resort to authoritarian types of teaching. They believe in the arts and skills of music and want to pass these on to others. To accomplish this, they keep their students disciplined and rigidly focused on the attainment of skills such as memory, analysis, and muscular dexterity.

When a teacher is democratic and humanitarian, on the contrary, he expects the student to be fully functioning in the here and now. He asks provocative questions. He satisfies student questions by breaking down the problems they pose into smaller questions. He expects the student to reason, compare, interpret, and create by using his higher powers of judgment and critical thinking.

Furthermore, a teacher who is democratic tries to develop within the student a system of inner controls so he can become self-directed. Because a student becomes highly motivated and ambitious when he begins to feel the joy of achieving through self-direction, the burden of teaching eases. A teacher can endure much more stress from misbehavior or inconvenience when students are working enthusiastically at their own improvement.

A democratic, humanistic teacher is able to instill a love for learning because he has first given an example of openness and has won the respect of the student. By observing the student's verbal and nonverbal cues the teacher gains insights about him. Because he perceives somewhat accurately the cognitive and emotional framework of each unique student, he can plan educational objectives which are meaningful and fulfilling to each class. He is student-oriented in his objectives and his procedures as well as in his evaluations of his teaching. He does not ask, "Does my chorus lack good blend?" Rather, he thinks of the educational development going on in each person of his chorus and asks himself, "Are my choral students listening for blend? Are they experiencing each other's voices as they sing?"

Democratic procedures leave a student free to explore, create, interpret, and enjoy music in his own natural way. The learner, having been helped to see the use of his higher talents and skills, feels intense motivation to use them. Stress tolerance in both student and teacher is heightened when learning behavior becomes spontaneous.

Confirming the Role of Teacher-Facilitator

Teachers who succeed know their role and adapt to the function they design for themselves. Students of behavior—Carl Rogers is

173

one—have described the role of the humanistic educator as a facilitator who acts as a catalyst in speeding up the union of the learner and knowledge. The humanistic teacher exposes the student to learning; then he stands back and allows the student to absorb knowledge and skills.[10]

Because music is a specialty, an art, and a discipline, however, the music educator is not only a facilitator. He must, because of the nature of his subject, do some lecturing, demonstrating, setting of standards, and establishing of evaluative criteria. Therefore, I see the music educator as a teacher-facilitator.

Music students need teachers who tell them things; they also need freedom from the interference of others when they want to discover deeper meanings for themselves. Unlike students of history, for instance, the music student cannot gain his knowledge simply by reading, discussing, observing and verifying. Books are often an inadequate source of information. Because music students are so different from each other in levels of achievement, talent, and tastes, they cannot share their musical experiences as their peers share their educational insights and encounters.

Although the subject of music limits the extent to which a teacher can use the role of facilitator, the music student gets his most significant knowledge from discovering it himself. For instance, a child may have taken private lessons for years before he suddenly discovers for himself the principles of staff and keyboard correlation. It is not uncommon for a student to experience a breakthrough and begin to read rapidly because an underlying principle has suddenly and excitingly become his.

The facilitator-teacher does not think *for* the student or *about* him but mainly *with* him. If at all possible, he prefers taking the stance of a co-searcher who asks questions to challenge the thinking powers of the student. Such a music teacher is like a nozzle on a garden hose which controls the flow of water and determines its direction.[11] A facilitator is concerned that the flow of knowledge with which the student grapples is neither too challenging nor too meaningless. He evaluates his procedures by asking himself questions such as, Is this what the student really needs to learn? Is he able to absorb this into his frame of reference? Does this challenge him sufficiently? Do these activities raise his morale and his self-esteem?

> There can be no significant innovation in education that does not have as its center the attitudes of teachers. The beliefs and assumptions of teachers *are* the learning atmosphere, and teachers determine the quality of life within it.[12]

In music education the role of the facilitator is to lay before the student the chance to identify rationally and emotionally with the art of musical expression. By creating a healthy atmosphere of empathy and enthusiasm, he furthers the student's personal involvement with the skill and meaning of music.

Students do not principally need people who tell them things. They need people to help them build themselves. They are not born with an adult sense of responsibility, but with help they can develop a certain amount of self-direction that enables them to teach themselves. Today many patterns in the home and outside it inhibit the child from feeling a personal sense of importance or power. A child from a push-button home lives in mother's house and has no feeling of ownership or family pride. It is not surprising that such children lack initiative in music class. They need someone to help them find their power of achievement.

Many students lag and underachieve, too, because of an unconscious or conscious rebellion against parental authority. By *not* learning an instrument, by *not* succeeding, a child can show his ability to stand on his own and win the battle against his parents. Facilitators who work with children can quite easily detect this attitude when planning procedures and goals with them. Students who plan for and seek goals enthusiastically differ markedly from those who only pretend they want to succeed.

A facilitator* changes, if possible, the pattern of self-mistrust or

---

* Further references to role of the teacher-facilitator are shortened simply to facilitator.

inner rebellion in the student through his techniques of interrelating. If a student comes to believe in himself and his ability to learn and change, there is a gradual increase of meaning and thrust in his life. If, on the contrary, students are troubled and confused, teachers should confront them in honest acceptance and talk together and plan for a solution to their problems. A music instructor need not make a farce out of the music program by continuing to fake his way through, believing he is doing his best when in reality he is not brave enough to address himself to the actual causes of student unrest and failure.

A genuine facilitator will see and take care of areas where the learning process is stymied. Because he operates with openness and warmth, he can encourage significant growth in people. Inobtrusive contact with his own inner genuine feelings stimulates honesty in his students. With respectful, yet firm, interaction with a student, a facilitator dispels or, at least, reduces the obstacles to learning in his class.

> Alexander the Great once asked the great
> Diogenes what he could do for him. "Stand out of
> my light!" was the reply.

Guiding Toward Self-Direction

Provided that negative forces in the learning environment are removed, the student will naturally want to grow and increase his potential. Very few people believe this. They constantly seek new methods and materials to "make" the student want to learn. Yet there is sufficient evidence to support the theory of innate urge toward self-enhancement. A facilitator does not need to motivate. The student needs only freedom and release from obstacles in order to learn.[13]

In a suitable climate of freedom and personal security there is an extraordinary possibility for the development of wholeness in a person. A climate of stimulation and human understanding opens the door to self-directed learning, which makes, in turn, a significant *difference* in the student.

The responsibility for learning grows from within. The spirit of inquiry often brings a sense of duty and energy to a student. When he feels drawn and attracted to a goal, the student becomes capable of hours of exhausting and tedious work. At times a student who fails miserably in music class may drop out and become extremely successful in popular music. An example of this is the folk hero Bob Dylan, who, after being dropped as a university student, found meaning and success perfecting his style without the help of music educators. Likewise, there are students who abandon their music classes and join rock groups where they find fulfillment of their immediate needs. Should music educators be broader in their scope? Should they be able to coach students in all styles of music?

You never make a good impression until you stop thinking about the sort of impression you are making.[14]

Creating an Atmosphere of Success

The role of a teacher is largely that of creating a climate conducive to study. The standards, the attitudes, the physical presence of a loving and caring teacher constitute the framework enclosing a student in his music study. What a teacher demands, allows, forbids, or enthusiastically supports form the perimeter within which a student develops himself musically.

A teacher-facilitator is like a farmer. He knows that he will reap a successful harvest only if he employs the arts of cultivation. He is like a biologist who places his cultures in an atmosphere of growth. He is also like a therapist in that he tries to create an atmosphere of safety and personal acceptance.

Upon entering a classroom or studio, a visitor can often quickly evaluate the atmosphere. The diligence and enthusiasm of the students as well as the alertness and assurance of the teacher are noticeable positive features. One might say that an atmosphere is best when the students are productively busy but the teacher, although he is perceptive and supportive, is relatively idle, waiting for his students to make their own discoveries.

The emotional tone of the atmosphere is often its most significant factor. The optimistic attitude of a success-oriented teacher can actually set the music program on fire. It is a kind of banked fire, harnessed to produce power personally and through students. As the enthusiastic teacher performs with vivid color, contrasting dynamics, and deep personal conviction, the world of music looks most attractive to students. The fire of a teacher's music-communication lights many other fires in students' lives.

The "as if" principle of William James can apply to music students who, when they aim at success, act as if they already have it. Persons—both teacher and student—who are reasonably sure of themselves and are enthusiastic about their music are powerful. By seeing themselves and others realistically and by believing in personal potential, they maintain a successful climate of study.

A successful music educator is a pillar of strength and inventiveness who, having struggled and won, can bring relief to the learner. He considers himself a flexible resource to be utilized by the group or by the individual student. He is always available as advisor, friend, or just as an experienced person. A facilitative teacher wants to be used as a resource, a springboard to self-directed learning. His answers often become questions which stimulate growth-motivating experiences in students. A friend to both the world of people and of research in music and music education, the catalyst-teacher is ever ready to try to help solve today's problems.

Yet there are always new situations, and yesterday's solutions do not fit today's problems. There are no absolutely correct answers in either the management of classes or the aesthetics of music. Thus, the music educator is constantly searching, seeking new evidence, and changing his temporary answers.

Making Resources Available

Because a successful teacher bases his procedures on the self-actualizing tendency in the normal person, he does not need to impose learning on students. Therefore, after establishing a stimulating atmosphere and creating an ambitious attitude, a teacher can "turn 'em loose" into the field of resources and allow students to teach themselves.

Students' self-directed study leads to discovery and personally appropriated learning—the only kind which is deep or lasting. Discoveries of aesthetic values, relationships, and the communicative power of music are so intimate and personal that they cannot be communicated. The really important aspects of music cannot be told; they must be experienced. Each person must, in a sense, reinvent these realities.

Once a truth is experienced, an empathic teacher should be there to accept, appraise, and evaluate the wealth which the student has amassed. When the teacher sees a student who is really excited over his discovery, he discusses it frankly with the student. If he sees that the student has gone wrong, the caring teacher asks a few questions through which the student sees his mistake. Because the student feels the warm acceptance of the teacher, the risk of correcting such a student is minimal.

One of the most important qualities of the successful teacher is his resourcefulness. He knows his music materials and keeps in touch, judicially, with new approaches to meet the needs of his students. Above all, he knows when to inspire his students and when to nurture them, when to be a loving parent and when to rule, more or less, with an iron hand. He knows when to lecture and when to question. He knows the kind of loving attention which is conducive to growth in students and the type of permissiveness which ruins them.

Student to His Students

"The door to his office is always open," writes Jenee Sinkule about her band director.[15] She goes on to say that his whole program of openness and approachability is the secret of his success. Other anecdotes of "my favorite teacher" invariably point up the tendency in highly accepted teachers to be empathic and open. The "we are in this together" leveling of roles brings out the best in students.

Because of the turbulence in music styles today, all teachers are, necessarily, learners. They constantly ask such questions as: What is good music? What about those new musical groups? How do we analyze them? If they spent several hours each day keeping up with contemporary developments in music, teachers might be authorities in their area. But, in reality, most educators can hardly survive the teaching day. They need students to help them learn the world of music in which they live. Because young people invariably experience modern music more vividly than adults, teachers need to learn from them.

The give-and-take attitude of a teacher in rapport with his students stimulates the atmosphere of learning. When little Carl tells me about the Twins and I learn from him about batting averages and shutouts, he feels my readiness to learn. Then I help him to learn about the athletic dimensions of his performance. There are few attitudes so threatening to a student as to constantly see himself in a totally different capacity than his teacher. A teacher who refers to himself as a learner and thanks his students for helping him learn more has success in store for him.

One characteristic of good mental health is flexibility. Opposite to flexibility is the negative trait rigidity. Successful music educators feel secure enough inside to reach out to types of music and procedures with which they have never worked before. They do not feel the need to cling to beliefs and practices which were taught to them in college. Although changes frighten them to some extent, they are open and ready for new insights. Progress for them means constant change. Nothing is permanent in music except a slow but constant changing of ideas, mediums, and goals.

> I have come to a frightening conclusion. I am the decisive element in the classroom . . . I can be a tool of torture or an instrument of inspiration. . . . In all situations it is my response that decides whether . . . a child [is] humanized or not.[16]

Aiming High

A successful music educator accomplishes his objectives, achieves his goals, and fulfills the mission of his role to a satisfactory degree. Because each teacher selects goals which are appropriate to his orientation and to his unique teaching situation, success embraces many aspects of musical experience. Music educators, writing about their craft, differ from each other in their statements about the components of successful teaching. Richard Chronister, for instance, implies the goals of the performance-oriented teacher when he writes:

> What makes a piano teacher really professional is his product—his students. If a teacher's students can read notes, play rhythmically, interpret convincingly, etc., then the teacher has succeeded—and is professional and should take great satisfaction in it.[17]

Charles Leonhard addresses himself to goals in these words:

> The basic mission of the music educator is to open the door to aesthetic experience and to nurture the aesthetic potential through exciting affective and meaningful experiences with music.[18]

Robert Klotman represents a more broad, humanistic viewpoint:

> Music is an art and a discipline involving aesthetic artistic judgment . . . we need teachers who are artists, scientists and humanists.[19]

The Tanglewood Symposium stated these goals:

> Educators must accept the responsibility for developing opportunities which meet many individual needs and the needs of a society plagued by the consequence of changing values, alienation, hostility between generations, racial and international tensions, and the challenges of a new leisure.[20]

This last statement envisions music education for the whole child, nurturing in him balanced growth and leading him to become a fully functioning human being.

Each educator has the privilege of holding to his own values and seeking the goals and rewards he esteems. Although he may shift pragmatically in pursuing his objectives, he remains essentially either geared to performance or dedicated to the broad education of the whole person of his student.

Success for the Performance-Oriented Teacher

The teacher who is basically oriented toward performance can easily evaluate the level of skill acquired by his students. Checking metronomic speeds in scale playing, giving sight-reading tests, and listening to old and recent tape recordings of student playing can be tools of evaluation. Contests and other competitions are valuable opportunities of measuring one's teaching of skill. When performances are compared, the fluency, flexibility, and virtuosity of students is obvious. However, the teacher usually knows before he enters the student that he is successful. Skill is not hard to detect.

The performance-oriented teacher experiences failure in two ways. In spite of effort, his students may not acquire skill. They may also drop out. They may come to feel as the Gryphon did in Lewis Carroll's book: "That's the reason they're called lessons; because they lessen from day to day." When students do not perform well the teacher who aims solely at performance can become discouraged, upset, and furiously angry, as well as, perhaps, financially poorer.

Because he wants to lure students to him and keep them within his music program, a teacher may adopt the "nice person" mask and effectively charm the students into practicing and liking the discipline of learning to play. A certain kind of relationship exists which enables the student to master his personal sluggishness and acquire some musical skill. However, so long as the focus of the program is fixed on superficial skills such as reading, dexterity, and speed, the educative effect can be very shallow. Students can become technical giants (or monsters) but remain personally and even musically immature.

> Creativity is largely an outgrowth of attitude
> rather than an activity, a set of predispositions
> rather than a production line.[21]

Success in Higher-Level Tasks

Educators who aim at producing key punchers and brilliant, showy performers can achieve success with only a very low level of rapport. They can insist on a specified series of drills and exercises aimed at achieving mechanical precision. The response of students is mechanical.

Higher-level tasks such as creativity and artistic coloration of tones and interpretation usually require a keener relationship between student and teacher. Because the teacher who aims at these higher skills has a unique task with each student, he must relate well to each individual. Here the problem of music education is not just the manipulation of an instrument, but the governing of one's inner speech. The task of educating includes knowing a student's feelings and personal aesthetics. It is releasing the expressive powers of this particular person in the form of a truly musical experience. The significant educator, the facilitator, is one who serves as a catalytic agent bringing about the union of music and a unique human being. The significant changes made by a person-centered music educator can be measured more by the quality of ideas and attitudinal enrichment than by the quantity of music literature studied.[22]

> One of the reasons most of us have lost the
> ability to create artistically is that we are covered
> with too many layers, too many years of pre-
> tending.[23]

Success in Creativity

Musical performance as expressive communication is essentially creative. A student needs to know his inner timing, his inner feelings, as well as to have an expansive view of the universe (ideas of unity, symmetry, contrast) in order to be able to relate to music creatively.

Creativity or spontaneity is a high-level music activity which can easily exist in the freeing environment where a teacher is in rapport with his students. Creativity here means a simple naturalness and free use of notes and rhythm to express oneself. This process, although a high-level task, is available to even a young child. Creativity is a talent found in all people who can form words into sentences and naturally use some vocal inflection. Maslow believes that creativity is largely an "innocent freedom of perception, an . . . uninhibited spontaneity and expressiveness."[24] He believes that these qualities are found in happy, secure children as well as in those adults who have not limited their freedom and vision with stereotypes or inhibitions.

A vital prerequisite for creativity is freedom. Insecurity and fear do not breed originality. Teachers who excel in relating to their students are able to create an atmosphere conducive to creativity. This freedom is such a key factor that it is probably more essential than talent. Freedom releases whatever a student or teacher has. In a free situation the teacher-facilitator builds a certain independence in students. Once a person is an independent creator, he trusts his "organic wisdom" and needs not fear that the threat of outer evaluation may destroy his composition or creative interpretation. He simply asks, "Does it satisfy *me?* Does it express *me?*" Certainly his performance must be true to the spirit of the composer whose music he is playing, but he does not really speak with other people's tongues—he has only the power to express his own feelings with his own spiritual and physical equipment.

Not only does a person relate well to his inner self when creating; he also loses his attachment to tradition and fixed patterns. He sees a possibility of how things *could be* and forgets, momentarily, how they *are*. He willingly divorces himself from the past and sets out to create a fresh combination of sounds which will surprise and delight him. Freely he has detached himself from old forms so as to be able to create new contrasts, new musical meanings.

Rapport between teacher and student nurtures the growth of personal integrity in the student. The creative student becomes "in tune" with his best self. To some extent he knows his deep feelings, is aware of his angers and selfish desires as well as of his deep desire and irresistible urge to express these concerns. He has access to the full richness of his emotional and intellectual experiences and integrates them for the building of a new creative expression of his total self. The creator is an open person who is tolerant of his thoughts even though they are conflicting, ambiguous, or vague. He is open to color and any medium which could be recreated and evolve into an original arrangement of the elements of music.

The act of creating is one of the most ecstatic joys of a human being. Words cannot describe the supreme joy of saying, "I've got it! I have discovered it! This music is my own inner speech!"

> A student who catches a glimmer of an exciting experience, such as having his own composition performed by a group, seeks the information that will make that vision a reality.[25]

Facilitating Creativity

The programs of instruction in most schools and studios are so highly specialized and structured that they usually dampen the students' interest in creating. Too often the requirements are so objective and burdensome that the student begins to see music as an "outside of me" phenomenon.

Before facilitating creativity, the teacher begins to alter the attitudes of students. A creative teacher does not consider music classes to be feeding stations or museums where certain bits of learning are collected and displayed. While he is trying to minimize academic hang-ups, the facilitator of creativity is alert to unusual questions or imaginative, creative brainstorms. If the student is to create, the idea must come from him, not wholly from the teacher.

Exercises are most helpful when creativity is just budding. To ask the students to convey a particular mood or character in sound and to accept the response, no matter how strange it might be, is to nurture a desire for creativity. The freeing of a student from the score is the first step to getting him to "speak" his own music. The score is the focus of attention in too many music education activities. The successful music educator believes that music is a phenomenon of sound. The medium through which sound is perceived is the ear, not the eye. Music is not black spots on paper. Music is an entity perceived by the ear. It is a communicative expression which one human being creates within his soul. It is an emotional message picked up by another's ear.

Sublime as it may be to create and have creative students, it is difficult to know how to handle creativity. No teacher feels comfortable when he is "snowed under" by too many compositions. He had best turn to other ways of building creative habits. Leaders of performing groups can develop the creative potential in students by having them conduct the group. Piano teachers can dramatize at the piano and stimulate the students to use the piano as a tool for telling stories. Many instrumental students feel their inner feelings in their fingertips and like to create spontaneously. Teenagers are usually excited by the contrasts they can get in various touches, tonguings, and breathing techniques.

Creativity can also take the form of playing "by ear." Playing by ear, if it is truly the ear that is doing most of the functioning, requires a concentration and mental alignment of phrases, dynamics, and internal lines within the music. It demands that one move at a steady pace without stopping.

Jazz players who play by ear and create spontaneously develop a high degree of musicianship. What are the elements in gaining such musicianship? The student must have good ego strength. He must believe in himself and his power to create. He must experience freedom in expressing himself before he can learn the rules and techniques involved. In all of this he needs sensitive guidance and an ability to conform to it.

Another medium of creativity is improvisation. When a student improvises, he plays without premeditation. The student who "feels" the ability and the urge to play needs only the activity in order to improve his style. Needing privacy, students usually find a basement or a lonely stage on which to experiment.

Many directors have adopted certain warm-up practices to provide a springboard for student improvisation. Some textbooks now introduce improvisation early in the course of study. At times this can result in almost intolerable noise. However, it can lead students to improvisatory techniques which they can enjoy the rest of their lives.

The strong argument for improvisation is that music is a communication system. If music is a language, why use other people's sentences in speaking? Who does not have a mood when he wants to express himself? If music teachers are educating people and freeing them to express themselves through music, improvisation, or creativity, is essential. There certainly are many reasons why people use written, composed music. But there need not be the slavish adherence to written scores which prevails in music education today—at least in this author's opinion.

Creativity is quite unnatural in a performance-oriented atmosphere. Most classrooms and studios in America today do not provide a healthy, free, trusting, and empathic climate for bursts of insight and fumbling creativity. Parents and teachers pay lip service to creativity but, ironically, provide an atmosphere which pays high premiums for conformity and effectively destroys creative qualities of intuition, curiosity, and invention. The weight of social custom and parental expectations can effectively smother all impulses to higher-level skills. That creativity continues to develop in some students is a credit to the accepting teacher who respects the student more than the music he plays. The tolerance such teachers practice could be a by-product of a sense of humor. As Gustav Holst once said, "If a thing is worth doing at all, it is worth doing badly." This creativity, of course, may also be due to a real drive in students—a drive that makes him overcome obstacles in his environment which prevent him from expressing himself creatively.

> If we have hope for our children that they will
> become full human beings and that they will
> move toward actualizing the potentialities that
> they have, then, as nearly as I can make out, the
> only kind of education in existence today that has
> any kind of faint inkling of such goals is art
> [aesthetic] education.[26]

187

There is an adage which warns that beauty is in the eye of the beholder. By the "eye" of the person is symbolized his entire self-image, connectedness, his experiences, attitudes, and values. It is his "inner time" which creates the scene in which the work of art finds its setting for that person. The person who listens to, composes, or performs a piece conceives of art as a mode of communication for himself. In a free atmosphere the student discovers that music speaks what his soul, his whole being is trying to say.

It is essential that the teacher-facilitator release the student from prejudice and bias and free him for the enjoyment of aesthetic beauty. Rather than establish rigid standards of "good" and "bad," the music teacher should sensitize the student to qualities of sound and organization. By increasing perception and awareness of definite aspects of an art experience, the teacher assures involvement on the part of the students. By participating in the evaluation of beauty, students develop a set of values which is deeply personal.

But teachers cannot sensitize their students to the perception of aesthetic values if they (1) use inferior music, (2) squelch students' statements of taste, or (3) lecture about music rather than give experience with music.[27] Teachers often want to teach literature and not aesthetics. They want to teach Bach or some rock. They want to teach music, not beauty. As long as they do not focus on the process within the human being of responding to beauty, students will simply learn to take on the values of others and call them their own.

Since there is pluralism in society today, the necessity of giving students the tools of analysis and aesthetics is most urgent. The arts are constantly undergoing change. All people need to begin to broaden their range of appreciation. To put it another way, music educators need to abandon the tunnel vision which tends to obliterate the music world on all sides of them. If they are to survive, they must be able to see aesthetic beauty where it is and not just where they want it to be.

Aesthetics does not involve complicated analysis of music. A student once wrote:

> O tell me the beauty of a melody.
> Speak not of its form to me
> Waste not on me a lengthy explanation of the harmonic series.
> It is more than that . . .
> Must a melody be analyzed?[28]

This young student perceived that it was by listening to a melody and intuitively knowing its meaning that he increased his aesthetic awareness. Melody for people like John is beauty which, in itself, makes emotional and intellectual sense.

> For the vast majority of us all the sacred cows have been shot. Youth will not be *told* what is beautiful.[29]

Can Aesthetics Be Taught?

The reader may ask, "But can I teach a system of aesthetic values and judgments?" The answer is, "No." A teacher cannot communicate a taste and desire for aesthetic beauty by talking about them. However, he can guide a student to greater understanding of the elements of art by dealing with assumptions, presumptions, and criteria expressing meanings and aesthetic values. He can be open to all kinds of art and be a comrade and fellow searcher with students, having empathy for them in their struggle to establish priorities in aesthetic values. Often teachers possess a keener sensitivity to aesthetic stimulation; frequently, on the other hand, students are more open to areas where teachers find bias and prejudice within themselves. At times the teacher's attempt to acquire a broadness of vision is a key factor which helps the student to eradicate his fear of being fooled by the values of his teacher.

While experts argue about whether or not educators are ready for the initiating of aesthetic programs into public schools, there remains one fundamental truth. If a fully alive teacher is immersed in the aesthetic beauty of music and this person is also in authentic communication with his students, he cannot help transfering a love for aesthetic beauty. A taste for soul-enriching experiences and a desire to look deeply into the meanings of music are values which are caught, not taught.

Interpretation

There are many valuable aspects of music which no one can really teach. Interpretive skill is one of those top-priority items which is ninety-five percent struggle and work on the part of a performer. The kind of interpretation referred to here is the intensive planning, critical listening, and keenly skilled control in playing or singing a musical piece.

It is quite safe to say that most students do not play with original interpretation. They pay little attention to what or how they play. They resemble, to some degree, robots being programmed by the musical composition. They wait for further direction from the teacher to set them in motion. They find it safer not to make any decisions or show their personality in a carefully planned, personal interpretation.

An effective teacher tries to involve the student in decisions about interpretation. By trying to engage the student in active listening, he guides the student to develop a new dimension to his art. Interpretation is an outgrowth of the discovery of the variety of sound and the marvels of musical combinations.

> In aesthetic experience the emotions function
> cognitively.[30]

Listening

The most important time in which to teach listening is that of early childhood. If children are keenly receptive to sound, the rewards of aesthetic enjoyment perpetuates such behavior. But it can be taught and encouraged beyond childhood, too. When a student of any age experiences good musical sounds, his listening is both a joy and a caution to correct performance. Listening provides tools for all musical activities. If, unfortunately, a student is neglected in this area, a great deal of listless playing will continue between spurts of good listening.

Critical listening is necessary for maximum progress in music. What are the stages or levels of efficient listening? Ramon Ricker compiled a list of nine stages. Students can be helped to hear (1) wrong notes, improper rhythms, (2) acceptable tone; (3) intonation; (4) "popped out" notes in legato phrases; (5) extra notes; (6) false notes in legato slur; (7) phrasing; (8) vibrato; (9) various intonations and temperaments, to which they then are able to adjust. Mr. Ricker believes that, although teachers listen at the final level, most students, unfortunately, stop their critical listening at the first.[31]

> In our investigations of peak experiences, we
> found many, many triggers . . . that would set
> them off. Apparently all people, or almost all
> people, have peak experiences, or ecstasies.[32]

Peak Experiences

Whether one is a small child totally delighted with the rhythmic movement of his body or an artist lost in the flow of a long musical phrase, the ecstasy of delight is, for the moment, complete. Music, Maslow believes, can be a fundamental means by which the total person expresses himself. According to him, if educative processes were directed toward "peak experiences," music programs could not be considered frills added to the curriculum superficially.[33]

In the area of peak experiences the teacher cannot lead the student where he has not gone himself. If I, for example, dash into the band room late for class and unprepared with new materials, the class can be interesting and successful in a skill-drill sort of fashion—if my luck is good. However, there will be no ecstasy in our music that day. Moreover, if there are relational problems in the class between students or between the students and the teacher, peak experiences are unlikely.

Yet peak experiences are natural. They are the sheer enjoyment and expressive spilling over of a human heart. A child or adult is filled with the wonder, the vastness, the beauty of the world. To a performer, a peak experience can mean that he loses awareness of his instrument, of his fingers, and of himself. Suddenly his soul, his deepest soul, is creating transcendent tonal beauty.

What happens when a person enjoys music so much that he transcends the things of this world? He is experiencing a different level of consciousness. The states of consciousness in people are like a "many-storied skyscraper." From the first floor, normal consciousness, a person can feel, see, think, solve problems, work, remember, and communicate. Many other things he can do on a lower and higher level—he can create, dream, and receive insight.[34]

Some who deal with peak experience describe it as a release from ego hang-ups and the tenacity with which a person clings to his possessions. Freed of fears and possessiveness, one somehow senses the transcendent clearly because his attachment to things is no longer keeping him earthbound. It is self-evident that one can deal with the arts more genuinely when stripped of ego involvements. A performer whose whole consciousness is filled with worries about people, events, and things, certainly is not able to express himself as a musician or a human being. Though he need not forget his distractions to the extent of entering another state of consciousness, being free of ego hang-ups does help in enabling him to fix his attention on his musical expression.

The premise here is simply that one can detach oneself from fears and worries partially by becoming a self-accepting, genuinely human person. An ego-centered person is a thing, not a self-actualizing human being. An artist who can transcend his conscious states if he wishes can interpret his music more creatively than one who is all tied up in selfish jealousy, anger, and other negative emotions.

It is not only the virtuoso who can experience music in the form of a peak experience. Children, too, can relax while listening to music. When they fix their attention on the music, they can forget their surroundings and experience a heightened awareness of musical sounds. Listening in such an altered state of consciousness can greatly enhance children's taste for music.[35]

> The arts . . . are so close to our psychological
> and biological core that . . . they must become
> basic experiences in education.[36]

Music and Human Living

What is the relationship between the pulse of human life and the dynamism of music? Could music be the mere extension of the human being? Which activities and features of music run parallel to the activities one experiences as a human being? Harold Zabrack, famous pianist, composer, and teacher, has conducted encounter groups researching and probing this question.[37]

After Zabrack and his group of musicians and psychologists relax and sit for a while in silence, they begin to realize that their most essential human activity is breathing. Then, after concentrating on the alternation between inhaling (which creates a tension inside the lung) and exhaling (which releases it), they begin to look for its musical counterpart. They find it in the tension-release patterns in music. As a musical phrase heightens to its emotional climax, a person experiences the tension of holding one's inhaled breath. Then, as the drama of the musical climax relaxes, the person experiences a release similar to that of exhalation. Other experiences in music also parallel this natural process.

The social system of unlike persons living together and complementing each other also has its corollary in music. In fact, all of society's role-enactment systems can be seen as parallel to the interplay of musical lines, melodic and rhythmic, occurring simultaneously during a musical performance.

That the pulse in music and the heartbeat within a human being relate to each other is obvious. However, when one considers that there are other organic pulses, such as peristalsis and cell regeneration, occurring at the same time but not in time with the pulse beat, one begins to realize that a complex, interactive system of counterpulsing has a corollary in the counterrhythms of contemporary music.

Placing musical compositions in their context reveals the extent to which musicians reflect and react to the spirit of their times. As man lived so he danced and sang. When living, other arts, and customs were elaborate, music was excessively ornate, with a tremendous activity and decorativeness. When the artistic and social customs were very proper, guarded, and elegant, the music of that age was marked with courtliness, restraint, and rigor. Later, after the Age of Reason and after the passions of the revolutionary wars, the musical style shifted to that of a turbulent, passionate romanticism. During the twentieth century, which has seen the monstrous usurpation of people's human rights and the reduction of humans to the level of things, music has become restless, dissonant, and barbaric in sound. And, of course, current technological achievements are reflected in ways of composing and performing. Today, as ever, music is the expression of the social man.

> Perhaps, instead of assuming that we have gone
> the education route and failed, it is more ac-
> curate to say that we have scarcely begun.[38]

Rapport and Success

What is rapport? What is success? These terms rightfully mean different and even opposing things to various professional people. Rapport varies from a patient tolerance bordering on frustration to a deep trusting relationship between student and teacher. The attitude of music educators toward success varies, too, from exterior precision and outward display to the highly personal involvement which students can have with music.

This book, however, considers as truly successful the music

educator who, as a person, is able to penetrate the humanness of his students and find meaningful music for them to express. Perceptive to his surroundings and to his own feelings, talents, and limits, he attempts realistic goals and achieves them. He knows that unless he fulfills his students' needs and satisfies their desire to communicate through music, he fails. Above all, the successful teacher aims at building his students into fully functioning human beings who can experience music as an outlet for their feelings as well as a source of aesthetic enjoyment for themselves and others.

Notes

1. Craig Harvey and Philip G. Zimbardo, "It's Tough to Tell a High School from a Prison," *Psychology Today* IX (June 1975), 30.

2. Thomas K. Cureton, "Health and Fitness in the Modern World and What Research Reveals," in *Physical Health for Educators,* David N. Aspy and Jane H. Buhler, eds. (Denton, Texas: North Texas State University Printing Office, 1975), p. 23.

3. *Ibid.*

4. Statement of David N. Aspy, speech at St. Francis High School, Little Falls, Mn., June 2, 1975.

5. David N. Aspy and June H. Buhler, eds., *Physical Health for Educators,* p. 1.

6. Alain, *Yoga for Perfect Health* (New York: Pyramid Books, 1957), p. 58.

7. David N. Aspy, Jane H. Buhler and William Brookshire, "A Study of a Method for Determining the Relationship between Physical Fitness as Measured by Heartbeats per Minute Recorded on the Physiograph and the Flanders Verbal Interaction Scale," in *Physical Health for Educators,* p. 110.

8. Ruth Stevenson Alling, *How to Make Money Teaching Piano to Beginners* (Corpus Christi, Texas: Ruth Alling Co., 1974), pp. 5-15.

9. R. E. Bowers and R. S. Soar, "Influence of Teacher Personality on Classroom Interaction," *Journal of Experimental Education* XXX (June 1962), 309-311.

10. See Carl Rogers, *Freedom to Learn* (Columbus, Ohio: Charles E. Merrill Publishing Co., 1969).

11. Robert Hilf, "Tailor-Made Music," *Clavier* XI (November 1972), 39-41.

12. Gerald F. Corey, *Teachers Can Make a Difference,* pp. 20-21.

13. Carl R. Rogers, *Freedom to Learn,* p. 199.

14. C. S. Lewis, *Beyond Personality, p. 68.*

15. Jenee Sinkule, "Why My Band Director Is the Greatest," *Selmer Student Bandwagon,* No. 10 (May 1974), p. 11.

16. Haim Ginott, *Between Teacher and Child*, pp. 15-16.

17. Richard Chronister, "What Makes an Independent Music Teacher Really Professional?" *Keyboard Arts* II (Spring 1973), p. 13.

18. Charles Leonard, "Human Potential and the Aesthetic Experience," *Music Educators Journal* 54 (April 1968), 33-41.

19. Robert H. Klotman, *The School Music Administrator and Supervisor: Catalysts for Change in Music Education,* p. 142.

20. "Tanglewood Symposium: Music in American Society," *Music Educators Journal* LIV (November 1967), 59.

21. Margery M. Vaughan, "Cultivating Creative Behavior," *Music Educators Journal* 59 (April 1973), 36.

22. Robert H. Klotman, p. 14.

23. Raymond C. Messler, Jr. "Arts and Man," *Music Educators Journal* 58 (February 1972), 39-42.

24. Abraham Maslow, *Toward a Psychology of Being* (New York: D. Van Nostrand Co., 1969), p. 138.

25. Roy Rummler, "Direct Involvement through Contemporary Composition: Practice Way to Force Feeding in General Music Class," *Music Educators Journal* 60 (December 1973), 23-25.

26. Abraham Maslow, "Music Education and Peak Experiences," *Music Educators Journal* 54 (February 1968), 72-75.

27. Charles H. Ball, "Thoughts on Music as Aesthetic Education," *Toward an Aesthetic Education* (Washington, D.C.: National Music Educators Conference, 1971), pp. 57-65.

28. James Croft, "Must a Melody Be Analyzed?" *Music Educators Journal* 60 (May 1974) 48-49.

29. N. U. Scarfe, "The Role of Education in Contemporary Society," *Gopher Music Notes* XXV (February 1969), 5-7.

30. Nelson Goodman, "Art and Understanding: The Need for a Less Simple-Minded Approach," *Music Educators Journal* 58 (February 1972), 43-45.

31. Ramon Ricker, "Developing Critical Listening in Private Clarinet Teaching," *The Instrumentalist* XXVII (March 1973), 70.

32. Abraham Maslow, "Music Education and Peak Experiences," p. 164.

33. *Ibid.,* p. 72.

34. Helen L. Bonny and Louis M. Savary, *Music and Your Mind* (New York: Harper & Row, Publishers, 1973), p. 13.

35. *Ibid.,* p. 138.

36. Abraham Maslow, "Music Education and Peak Experiences," p. 74.

37. Harold Zabrack, "The Musical Encounter Experience," *Clavier* XII (April 1973), 44-45.

38. John I. Goodlad, "Our Education System Corrupts the Human Spirit," *Music Educators Journal* 55 (December 1968), 30.

Bibliography

Allen, Dwight W., and Christiansen, Phillip. "Using Time, Space and People Effectively." In *Controversies in Education*. Philadelphia: W. B. Saunders Co., 1974.

Alling, Ruth Stevenson. *How To Make Money Teaching Piano to Beginners*. Corpus Christi, Texas: Ruth Alling Co., 1974.

Amidon, Edmund J., and Hough, John B. *Interaction Analysis: Theory, Research and Application*. Reading, Mass.: Addison-Wesley Publishing Co., 1967.

Anthony, W. S. "Learning to Discover Rules by Discovery." *Journal of Educational Psychology* 64, No. 3 (1973): 325-328.

_____. "How Did He Get There?" In *The Helping Relationship Sourcebook*, edited by Avila, Combs, and Purkey. Boston: Allyn & Bacon, 1971.

Aspy, David N. "The Effect of Teacher-Offered Conditions of Empathy, Congruence, and Positive Regard Upon Student Achievement." *Florida Journal of Educational Research* II (1969) 39-48.

_____. *Toward a Technology for Humanizing Education*. Champaign, Illinois: Research Press Co., 1972.

_____ and Hadlock, W. "The Effect of High and Low Functioning Teachers upon Students' Performance." In *Beyond Counseling and Therapy*, by Carkhuff, R. R., and Berenson, B. New York: Holt, Rinehart and Winston, 1967.

_____ and Roebuck, Flora N., "From Humane Ideas to Human Technology and Back Again Many Times." *Education* 95, no. 2 (November-December 1974): 163-171.

_____. "An Investigation of the Relationship Between Levels of Cognitive Functioning and the Teacher's Classroom Behavior." *Journal of Educational Research* 65 (May 1972).

Ausubel, D. P., and Robinson, F. G. *School Learning: An Introduction to Educational Psychology.* New York: Holt, Rinehart and Winston, 1962.

Austin, Virginia D. "Striking a Balance between Participation and Perfection," *Music Educators Journal* 60 (March 1974): 35.

Ball, Charles H. "Thoughts on Music as Aesthetic Education." In *Toward an Aesthetic Education.* Washington, D.C.: National Music Educators Conference, 1971.

Barbara, Dominik A. *Your Speech Reveals Your Personality.* Springfield, Ill.: Charles C. Thomas Co., 1958.

Barker, Larry L. *Listening Behavior.* Englewood Cliffs, N.J.: Prentice-Hall, 1971.

Barnes, D. "An Analysis of Remedial Activities Used by Elementary Teachers in Coping with Classroom Behavior Problems." *Journal of Educational Research* 56 (1963): 544-547.

Barron, B. *Creative Person and Creative Process.* New York: Holt, Rinehart and Winston, 1969.

Bastien, James W. *How to Teach Piano Successfully.* Park Ridge, Ill.: General Words and Music Co., 1973.

Beck, Joan. *How to Raise a Brighter Child.* New York: Simon & Schuster, 1975.

Beeler, Walter, and Hunsberger, Donald, et al., "The Band Conductor as Musician and Interpreter." *The Instrumentalist* 27, no. 9 (April 1973): 34-39.

Bell, Windell. "Social Science; the Future as a Missing Variable." *Learning for Tomorrow* edited by Alvin Toffler. New York: Random House Vintage Books, 1974.

Benner, Charles H. *Teaching Performing Groups: From Research to the Music Classroom.* No. 2. Washington, D.C.: Music Educators National Conference, 1972.

Berglund, Robert, "Meaning in Music," *Gopher Music Notes* 30, no. 2 (December 1973): 2-3.

Berman, Louise M. *New Priorities in the Curriculum.* Cleveland, Ohio: Charles E. Merrill Publishing Co., 1968.

Berne, Eric. *Games People Play.* New York: Random House, 1967.

───────────. *Transactional Analysis in Psychotherapy.* New York: Grove Press, 1961.

───────────. *What Do You Say After You Say Hello?* New York: Bantam Books, Inc., 1972.

Bigge, Morris L. *Learning Theories for Teachers.* 2nd ed. New York: Harper & Row, Publishers, 1971.

Bird, Joseph and Lois. *Power to the Parents!* Garden City, N.Y.: Doubleday, Co., 1972.

Blanchard, Kenneth H., and Hersay, Paul. "The Teacher as Leader." In *Controversies in Education.* Philadelphia: W. B. Saunders Co., 1974.

Bloom, Kathryn. "Development of Arts and Humanities Programs." In *Toward an Aesthetic Education.* Washington, D.C.: Music Educators National Conference, 1971.

Bonny, Helen L., and Savary, Louis M. *Music and Your Mind.* New York: Harper & Row Publishers, 1973.

Borton, Terry. *Reach, Touch and Teach.* New York: McGraw-Hill Book Co., 1970.

Bower, Gordon H. "How to . . . Uh . . . Remember!" *Psychology Today* 7, no. 5 (October 1973): 63-70.

Branden, Nathaniel. *Breaking Free.* Los Angeles: Nash Publishing Corp., 1970.

_____. *The Psychology of Self-Esteem.* Los Angeles: Nash Publishing Corp., 1969.

Bruner, Jerome S. *Of Knowing: Essays for the Left Hand.* Forge Village, Mass.: Murray Printing Co., 1962.

_____. *The Process of Education.* New York: Random House, Vintage Books, 1960.

_____. *The Relevance of Education.* New York: W. W. Norton & Co., 1971.

Buber, Martin. *I and Thou.* New York: Charles Scribner's Sons, 1958.

Buhler, June H. and Aspy, David N. *Physical Health for Educators.* Denton, Texas: North Texas State University Printing Office, 1975.

Burton, Gary. "Improvisation—for Basic Musicianship." *The Instrumentalist* 27, no. 8 (March 1973): 32.

Cappon, Clyde. "Learning to Listen, Listening to Learn." *Music Educators Journal* 55, no. 5 (January 1974): 40-45.

Carkhuff, Robert R. *Belly to Belly Back to Back.* Edited by Bernard G. Berenson. Amherst, Mass.: Human Resource Development Press, 1975.

_____ and Truax, Charles. "Toward Explaining Success and Failure in Interpersonal Learning Experience." In *The Helping Relationship Sourcebook.* Boston: Allyn & Bacon, 1971.

Carver, Fred D., and Sergiovanni, Thomas J., eds. *Organizations and Human Behavior.* New York: McGraw-Hill Book Co., 1969.

Casals, Pablo. "Life: A Fantasy with Music." In *They Talk about Music,* edited by Robert Cumming. Vol. 1. Rockville Centre, N.Y.: Belwin/Mills Pub. Corp., 1971.

Chronister, Richard. "What Makes an Independent Music Teacher Really Professional?" *Keyboard Arts* 2 (Spring 1973): 13.

Clark, Donald H., and Kadis, Asya L. *Humanistic Teaching.* Columbus, Ohio: Charles E. Merrill Publishing Co., 1971.

Coleman, James C. *Personality Dynamics and Effective Behavior.* Chicago: Scott, Foresman and Co., 1960.

Combs, Arthur W. "The Basic Concepts in Perceptual Psychology," "Fostering Self-Direction," "Intelligence from a Perceptual Point of View," and "What Can Man Become?" In *The Helping Relationship Sourcebook.* Boston: Allyn & Bacon, 1971.

Committee on Adolescence. *Normal Adolescence.* New York: Charles Scribner's Sons, 1968.

Corey, Gerald F. *Teachers Can Make a Difference.* Columbus, Ohio: Charles E. Merrill Publishing Co., 1973.

Crawford, Donald W. "Philosophical Aesthetics and Aesthetic Education." *Journal of Aesthetic Education* 2, no. 2 (April 1968): 37-49.

Croft, James. "Must a Melody be Analyzed?" *Music Educators Journal* 60, no. 9 (May 1974): 48-49.

Cronbach, Lee J. *Educational Psychology.* Chicago: Harcourt, Brace and Co., 1966.

Cross, Elsie Y., and Rosenstein, Irving. "Do Teachers Want What Students Need?" In *Controversies in Education.* Philadelphia: W. B. Saunders Co., 1974.

Curran, Charles A. *Religious Values in Counseling and Psychotherapy.* New York: Sheed & Ward, 1969.

——————. *Counseling and Psychotherapy.* New York: Sheed & Ward, 1968.

Cureton, Thomas K. "Health and Fitness in the Modern World and What Research Reveals." *Journal of Physical Education* 70 (September-October 1972): 239-243.

Deutsch, Diana. "Music and Memory." *Psychology Today* 1, no. 7 (December 1972): 87-89.

Dewey, John. *Art as Experience.* New York: Capricorn Books, 1958.

_____. *Experience and Education.* New York: Macmillan Publishing Co., 1938.

Doray, Maya B. *See What I can Do!* Englewood Cliffs, N.J.: Prentice-Hall, 1973.

Douglas, Mack R. *How to Make a Habit of Succeeding.* Grand Rapids, Mich.: Zondervan Corp., 1966.

Eaton, Manford L. "Induce and Control." *Music Educators Journal* 59, no. 5 (January 1973): 54-57.

Edelson, Edward. "Discover Music through the Creative Process," *The Instrumentalist* 28, no. 5 (September 1973): 36-37.

Ehlers, Henry. *Crucial Issues in Education.* Chicago: Holt, Rinehart and Winston, 1969.

Elkind, D. "Cognitive Development in Adolescence." In *Understanding Adolescence: Current Developments in Adolescent Psychology,* edited by J. F. Adams. Boston: Allyn & Bacon, 1968.

Faulkner, William. *The Bear.* New York: Random House, 1944.

Flanders, Ned. A. *Analyzing Teaching Behavior.* Reading, Mass.: Addison-Wesley Publishing Co., 1970.

Frankl, Viktor E. *Psychotherapy and Existentialism.* New York: Simon & Schuster, 1967.

Flavell, J. H. *The Developmental Psychology of Jean Piaget.* Princeton: D. Van Nostrand Co., 1963.

Frankl, Viktor E. *Psychotherapy and Existentialism.* New York: Simon & Schuster, 1967.

Fromm, Erich. *The Art of Loving.* New York: Harper & Bros., 1956.

_____. *The Revolution of Hope.* New York: Harper & Row, Publishers, 1971.

Funes, Donald J. "Expand! Expand! or Sometimes They Circle Classical." *Music Educators Journal* 60, no. 2 (October 1973): 52-55.

Furth, Hans G. *Piaget for Teachers.* Englewood Cliffs, N.J.: Prentice-Hall, 1970.

Gardener, John W. *Self-Renewal.* New York: Harper & Row, Publishers, 1964.

Gelvin, Miriam P. "Arts Experiences in Early Childhood Education." *Music Educators Journal* 60, no. 7 (March 1974).

Glasser, William. *Schools without Failure.* New York: Harper & Row, Publishers, 1965.

Gilles, Dorothy, and Kovitz, Valerie. "What to Do with the Learning Disabled." *Clavier* 12, no. 6 (September 1973): 14-17.

Ginott, Haim G. *Between Parent and Child.* New York: Avon Books, 1965.

_____. *Between Parent and Teenager.* New York: Avon Books, 1971.

_____. *Between Teacher and Child.* New York: Congruent Communications, 1972.

Ginsberg, Herbert, and Opper, Sylvia. *Piaget's Theory of Intellectual Development.* Englewood Cliffs, N.J.: Prentice-Hall, 1969.

Goble, Frank. *The Third Force.* New York: The Benjamin Company, 1970.

Goodlad, John I. "Our Education System Corrupts the Human Spirit." *Music Educators Journal* 55, no. 4 (December 1968): 30.

Goodman, Nelson. "Art and Understanding: The Need for a Less Simple-Minded Approach." *Music Educators Journal* 58 (February 1972): 43-45.

Gorney, Roderic. *The Human Agenda.* New York: Bantam Books, 1972.

Greenberg, Herbert M. *Teaching with Feeling.* New York: Pegasus, 1970.

Greene, Maxine, "Teaching for Aesthetic Experience." In *Toward an Aesthetic Education.* Washington, D.C.: Music Educators National Conference, 1971.

Greer, Mary, and Rubenstein, Bonnie. *Will the Real Teacher Please Stand Up?* Pacific Palisades, Calif.: Goodyear Publishing Co., 1972.

Groch, Judith. *The Right To Create.* Boslon: Little, Brown and Co., 1970.

Guilford, J. P. *Intelligence, Creativity and Their Implications.* San Diego: Knapp Publishing Co., 1968.

Hall, Edward T. *The Silent Language.* Garden City, New York: Doubleday & Co., 1959.

Hall, Elizabeth. "A Conversation with Jean Piaget and Barbel Inhelder." *Psychology Today* 4 (May 1970); 30.

Hamer, John H. "Communication with the Band." *The Instrumentalist* 27, no. 5 (December 1972): 58-59.

Harper, Andrew, et al. "Education Through Music." *Gopher Music Notes* 30, no. 2 (December 1973): 4-5.

Harris, Thomas A. *I'm OK—You're OK.* New York: Harper & Row, Publishers, 1969.

Harvey, Arthur W. "A Conductor in Every Chair." *Music Educators Journal* 58, no. 1 (September 1972): 46-47.

Harvey, Craig, and Zimbardo, Philip G. "It's Tough to Tell a High School from a Prison." *Psychology Today* 9 (June 1975): 30.

Hausman, Jerome J. "A Contemporary Aesthetics Curriculum." In *Toward an Aesthetic Education.* Washington, D.C.: National Music Educators Conference, 1971.

Havighurst, R. J. "Overcoming Value Differences." In *The Inner-City Classroom: Teacher Behaviors,* edited by R. Strom. Columbus, Ohio: Ohio State University Press, 1966.

Henderson, Robert W., ed. *Helping Yourself with Applied Psychology.* West Nyack, N.Y.: Parker Publishing Co., 1967.

Holt, John. *Escape from Childhood.* New York: Ballantine Books, 1974.

_____. "What You See Isn't Necessarily What You Get." *Music Educators Journal* 60, no. 9 (May 1974): 35-37.

Hoopes, Ned E., and Pack, Richard, eds. *The Edge of Awareness.* New York: Dell Publishing Co., 1966.

Horrocks, J. *Psychology of Adolescence.* Boston: Houghton Mifflin Co., 1969.

Hortshorn, William C. "The Musical Education of the Gifted." *Music Educators Journal* 54, no. 6 (February 1968): 76-78.

Jager, Robert. "Humanizing the Composer." *The Instrumentalist* 26, no. 11 (June 1972): 36.

James, Muriel, and Jongeward, Dorothy. *Born to Win.* Reading, Mass.: Addison-Wesley Publishing Co., 1971.

James, William. *Principles of Psychology.* New York: Dover Publications, 1950.

Jenkins, Harry. "Sight Reading—A Disaster Area." *The Instrumentalist* 27, no. 4, (November 1972): 16-17.

Jennings, F. G. "Jean Piaget: Notes on Learning." *Saturday Review,* May 20, 1967, pp. 81-83.

Jersild, Arthur T. *In Search of Self.* New York: Teachers College Press, Columbia University, 1952.

_____. *When Teachers Face Themselves.* New York: Teachers College Press, Columbia University, 1966.

Jourard, Sidney M., *The Transparent Self.* Princeton, N.J.: D. Van Nostrand Col., 1964.

Kagan, Jerome, *Understanding Children*. Chicago: Harcourt Brace Jovanovich, 1971.

Karlin, Muriel Schoenbrun, and Berger, Regina. *Discipline and the Disruptive Child: A Practical Guild for Elementary Teachers*. West Nyack, N.Y.: Parker Publishing Co., 1972.

Kelley, Earl C. "Another Look at Individualism." In *The Helping Relationship Sourcebook*. Boston: Allyn & Bacon, 1971.

Kirschenbaum, Howard, and Simon, Sidney B. *Values and the Future's Movement in Education*. New York: Random House, Vintage Books, 1974.

Klausmeier, Herbert J., and Ripple, Richard E. *Learning and Human Abilities*. New York: Harper & Row, Publishers, 1971.

Kleinke, Chris L. *First Impressions*. Englewood Cliffs, N.J.: Prentice-Hall, 1975.

Klotman, Robert H. *The School Music Administrator and Supervisor: Catalysts for Change in Music Education*. Englewood Cliffs, N.J.: Prentice-Hall, 1973.

Kneiter, Gerald. "The Nature of Aesthetic Education." In *Toward an Aesthetic Education*. Washington, D.C.: Music Educators National Conference, 1971.

Kohl, Herbert. *36 Children*. New York: New American Library, Signet Boosk, 1967.

Kolb, Lawrence C. *Modern Clinical Psychiatry*. Philadelphia: W. B. Saunders Co., 1973.

Komisar, B. Paul, and Macmillan, C. *Psychological Concepts in Education*. Chicago: Rand McNally & Co., 1967.

Ladd, Edward T. "Teachers as Cause and Cure of Student Unrest." In *Controversies in Education*. Philadelphia: W. B. Saunders Company, 1974.

LaFosse, Leopold. "Teaching the Art of Practicing." *The Instrumentalist* 26, no. 5 (December 1973): 42-43.

Laing, R. D.; Phillipson, H.; and Lee, A. R. *Interpersonal Perception*. New York: Harper & Row, Publishers, 1966.

Lair, Jess. *I Ain't Much, Baby—But I'm All I've Got*. Garden City, N.Y.: Doubleday & Co., 1972.

Lane, Howard, and Beauchamp, Mary. *Human Relations in Teaching*. Englewood Cliffs, N.J.: Prentice-Hall, 1955.

Langer, Susanne K. *Problems of Art*. New York: Charles Scribner's Sons, 1957.

206

Larson, Richard C. "Behaviors and Values: Creating a Synthesis. *Music Educators Journal* 60, no. 2 (October 1973): 41-43.

Lasker, Henry. *Teaching Creative Music in Secondary Schools.* Boston: Allyn & Bacon, 1971.

Lee, James Michael, and Pallone, Nathaniel. *Readings in Guidance and Counseling.* New York: Sheed & Ward, 1966.

Leonard, George. *Education and Ecstasy.* New York: Dell Publishing Co., Delta Books, 1968.

Leonhard, Charles. "Human Potential and the Aesthetic Experience." *Music Educators Journal* 54, no. 8 (April 1968); 33-41.

Lerner, Max. *Education and a Radical Humanism.* Columbus, Ohio: Ohio State University Press, 1962.

Leuba, Clarence. *Personality, Interpersonal Relations and Self-Understanding.* Columbus, Ohio: Charles E. Merrill Publishing Co., 1962.

Lifton, Walter M. *Working with Groups.* New York: John Wiley & Sons, 1966.

Lowen, Alexander. *The Betrayal of the Body.* New York: Macmillan Co., 1967.

Lyon, Harold D. Jr. *Learning to Feel—Feeling to Learn.* Columbus, Ohio: Charles E. Merrill Publishing Co., 1971.

Maher, Trafford P. *Self—A Measureless Sea.* St. Louis, Mo.: Catholic Hospital Association, 1966.

Maltz, Maxwell. *The Magic Power of Self-Image Psychology.* Englewood Cliffs, N.J.: Prentice-Hall, 1964.

——————. *Psychocybernetics.* New York: Essandess Special Editions, 1968.

——————. *Psycho-Cybernetics and Self-Fulfillment.* New York: Bantam Books, 1970.

Mainwaring, J. "The Meaning of Musicianship: A Problem in the Teaching of Music." *British Journal of Educational Psychology* 11 (1941).

Mancini, Henry. "Discover Music through Popular Music." *The Instrumentalist* 28 (September 1973): 32-33.

Marcus, Adele. "Creative Study and Practicing." *Clavier* 8, no. 1 (January 1969): 38-39.

Mark, Michael L. "Traditional Music—The Stabilizer That Helps Us Cope with Change." *Music Educators Journal* 60, no. 5 (January 1974): 46-48.

Maslow, Abraham H. "The Creative Attitude." *The Helping Relationship Sourcebook*. Boston: Allyn & Bacon, 1971.

_____. *The Farthest Reaches of Human Nature*. New York: Viking Press, 1971.

_____. *Motivation and Personality*. New York: Harper & Row, Publishers, 1954.

_____. "Music Education and Peak Experience." *Music Educators Journal* 54, no. 6 (February 1968): 72-75.

_____. "Self Actualization and Beyond." In *Human Dynamics in Psychology and Education,* edited by D. Hamashek. Boston: Allyn & Bacon, 1968.

_____. "Some Educational Implications of the Humanistic Psychologies." *Harvard Educational Review* 38, no. 4 (Fall 1969): 689.

_____. *Toward a Psychology of Being*. New York: D. Van Nostrand Co., 1968.

May, F. B. "Creative Thinking: A Factorial Study of Seventh-Grade Children." Unpublished doctoral dissertation. Madison, Wisc.: University of Wisconsin, 1961.

May, Rollo. *Love and Will*. New York: W. W. Norton & Co., 1969.

_____. *Man's Search for Himself*. New York: W. W. Norton & Co., 1953.

Mead, Margaret. "Youth Revolt: The Future Is Now." *Saturday Review,* January 10, 1970, pp. 23-24, 113.

Mehr, Norman. "Pointers from the School Classroom." *Clavier* 10, no. 2 (February 1971): 42-45.

Menninger, Karl. *Man Against Himself*. New York: Harcourt, Brace & World, 1938.

Mercer, J. Jack. "Is the Curriculum the Score—or More?" *Music Educators Journal* 58, no. 6 (February 1972): 50-53.

Messler, Raymond C., Jr. "Arts and the Man." *Music Educators Journal* 58, no. 6 (February 1972): 39-42.

Meyer, Leonard B. *Music, the Arts and Ideas*. Chicago: University of Chicago Press, 1967.

Mischel, Walter. *Introduction to Personality*. New York: Holt, Rinehart and Winston, 1971.

Montessori, Maria. *The Secret of Childhood*. New York: Ballantine Books, 1966.

_____. *The Absorbent Mind*. New York: Dell Publishing Co., 1967.

208

Moustakas, Clark. *The Authentic Teacher.* Cambridge, Mass.: Doyle Publishing Co., 1966.

—————. *The Child's Discovery of Himself.* New York: Ballantine Books, 1966.

—————. *Creativity and Conformity.* New York: Van Nostrand Reinhold, 1967.

—————. *Teaching as Learning.* New York: Ballantine Books, 1972.

Mursell, James L. *The Psychology of Music.* New York: W. W. Norton & Co., 1937.

Mussen, Paul Henry; Congar, John Janeway; Kagan, Jerome. *Child Development and Personality.* 4th ed. New York: Harper & Row, Publishers, 1974.

Neidlinger, Robert J. "Dimensions of Sound and Silence." *Music Educators Journal* 59, no. 8 (April 1973): 29.

Neilson, James. "The Competent School Band Conductor." *The Instrumentalist* 27, no. 7 (February 1973): 54-57.

Novik, Ylda. "Teaching Teens in the Weekly Piano Class." *Clavier* 12, no. 1 (January 1973): 33-35.

Novinson, Noel. "School Is Unconstitutional, 1962/1972." In *Controversies in Education.* Philadelphia: W. B. Saunders Company, 1974.

Ott, Pat Bernard. "Occupation: Child Teacher." *Clavier* 12, no. 1 (January 1973): 46-48.

Nadig, Henry D., Jr. "Some Behavioral Objectives for Teachers." *English Journal* 62, no. 3 (March 1974): 53-56.

Pace, Robert. *Teachers Manual.* Lee Roberts Music Publications, 1970.

Palisca, Claude V., "Music in our Schools: A Search for Improvement." Office of Education, U.S. Dept. of Health, Ed., and Welfare, Bulletin No. 28, 1964.

Patterson, C. H. "The Self in Recent Rogerian Theory." In *The Helping Relationship Sourcebook.* Boston, Mass.: Allyn & Bacon, 1971.

Peale, Norman Vincent. *Enthusiasm Makes the Difference.* Greenwich, Conn.: Fawce Publications, 1967.

Perls, Frederick. *Gestalt Therapy Verbatim.* Lafayette, California: Real People Press, 1969.

—————. *In and Out the Garbage Pail.* New York: Bantam Books, 1969.

Piaget, Jean. *The Child's Conception of Space.* New York: W. W. Norton & Co., Norton Library, 1967.

_____. *The Construction of Reality in the Child.* New York: Basic Books, 1954.

_____. *Six Psychological Studies.* New York: Random House, Vintage Books Edition, 1968.

Postman, Neil and Weingartner, Charles. *Teaching as a Subversive Activity.* New York: Dell Publishing Co., Delta Books, 1969.

Prestia, Ross J. "Reducing the Dropout Rate." *The Instrumentalist* 28, no. 1 (August 1972): 32-33.

Prescott, D. *The Child in the Educative Process.* New York: McGraw-Hill, 1957.

Purkey, William W. "The Task of a Teacher." In *The Helping Relationship Sourcebook.* Boston: Allyn & Bacon, 1971.

Raths, Louis E.; Harmin, Merrill; Simon, Sidney, B. *Values and Teaching.* Columbus, Ohio: Charles E. Merrill Publishing Co., 1966.

Read, Donald A., and Simon, Sidney B., eds. *Humanistic Education Sourcebook.* Englewood Cliffs, N.J.: Prentice-Hall, 1975.

Reese, Sam. "Discovering the Non-intellectual Self." *Music Educators Journal* 60, no. 9 (May 1974): 46-47.

_____. "New Music Breeds Creators, Not Repeaters." *Music Educators Journal* 59, no. 5 (January 1973): 65-67.

Reichert, Richard. *The Real Thing.* Notre Dame, Indiana: Ave Maria Press, 1972.

Reimer, Bennett. "Aesthetic Behaviors in Music." In *Toward an Aesthetic Education.* Washington, D.C.: National Music Educators Conference, 1971.

_____. "Developing Aesthetic Sensitivity in the Junior High School." *Journal of Aesthetic Education* 2, no. 2 (April 1968): 98.

_____. "Putting Aesthetic Education to Work." *Music Educators Journal* 59, no. 1 (September 1972): 30.

Rhodes, Joseph, Jr. "Student Freedom?" In *Controversies in Education.* Philadelphia: W. B. Saunders Co., 1974.

Richards, Mary Helen. "A Song in the Life of a Child." *Gopher Music Notes* 31, no. 2 (February 1974): 10-12.

Ricker, Ramon. "Developing Critical Listening in Private Clarinet Teaching." *The Instrumentalist* 27, no. 8 (March 1973): 70.

Robb, Margaret D. *The Dynamics of Motor-Skill Acquisition.* Englewood Cliffs, N.J.: Prentice-Hall, 1972.

Rogers, Carl R. *Carl Rogers on Encounter Groups.* New York: Harper & Row, Publishers, 1970.

_____. "The Characteristics of a Helping Relationship." In *The Helping Relationship Sourcebook.* Boston: Allyn & Bacon, 1971.

_____. *Client-Centered Therapy.* Boston: Houghton Mifflin Co., 1951.

_____. *Freedom to Learn.* Columbus, Ohio: Charles E. Merrill Publishing Co., 1969.

_____. "The Interpersonal Relationship in the Facilitation of Learning." In *The Helping Relationship Sourcebook.* Boston: Allyn & Bacon, 1971.

_____. *On Becoming a Person.* Boston: Houghton Mifflin Co., 1961.

_____. "The Person of Tomorrow." In *Will the Real Teacher Stand Up?* edited by Mary Green and Bonnie Rubenstein. Pacific Palisades, Calif.: Goodyear Publishing Co., 1972.

_____ and Stevens, Barry. *Person to Person.* New York: Simon & Schuster, Pocket Books, 1967.

_____. "Two Divergent Trends." In *Existential Psychology,* edited by Rollo May. New York: Random House, 1961.

Rosenthal, Robert, and Jacobson, Lenore. *Pygmalion in the Classroom.* New York: Holt, Rinehart and Winston, 1968.

Rosenthal, Robert. "The Pygmalion Effect Lives." *Psychology Today* 7, no. 4 (September 1973): 56-62.

Rummler, Roy. "Direct Involvement through Contemporary Composition: Practice Way to Force-Feeding in General Music Class." *Music Educators Journal* 60, no. 4 (December 1973): 23-25.

Satir, Virginia. *Peoplemaking.* Palo Alto, Calif.: Science and Behavior Books, 1972.

Scarfe, N. U. "The Role of Education in Contemporary Society." *Gopher Music Notes* 25, no. 3 (February 1969): 5-7.

Schmitt, Sr. Cecilia. "A Paradigm of Music Concepts." Unpublished thesis. Minneapolis, Minn.: University of Minnesota, 1971.

_____. "The Thought Life of the Young Child." *Music Educators Journal* 58, no. 4 (December 1971): 22-26.

Schneiders, Alexander A. *The Anarchy of Feeling.* New York: Sheed & Ward, 1963.

Schuman, William. "Cultivating Student Taste." *Today's Education* 57, no. 3 (November 1968): 11-13.

Seabury, David. *The Art of Selfishness.* New York: Simon & Schuster, Cornerstone Library, 1964.

Seashore, Carl E. *Psychology of Music.* New York: McGraw-Hill Book Co., 1938.

Snygg, Donald. "A Cognitive Field Theory of Learning." In *The Helping Relationship Sourcebook,* Boston: Allyn & Bacon, 1971.

_____. "The Psychological Basis of Human Values." In *The Helping Relationship Sourcebook.* Boston: Allyn & Bacon, 1971.

Silberman, Charles E. *The Open Classroom Reader.* New York: Random House, 1973.

Simon, Sidney B.; Howe, Leland W.; Kirschenbaum, Howard. *Values Clarification.* New York: Hart Publishing Co., 1972.

Smith, Susy. *ESP and You.* New York: Macfadden-Bartell Corp., 1972.

Starr, William. "A Look at the Suzuki Scene—1974." *American Suzuki Journal* 2, no. 2 (July 1974): 1-2.

Steinbeck, John. *East of Eden.* New York: Viking Press, 1952.

Steinberg, William. "The Function of a Conductor." In *They Talk about Music* Vol. 2. Edited by Robert Commings. Rockville Centre, N.Y.: Belwin/Mills Publishing Corp., 1971.

Stevens, John O. *Awareness: Exploring, Experimenting, Experiencing.* Moab, Utah: Real People Press, 1971.

Suzuki, Shin'ichi. *Nurtured by Love.* New York: Exposition Press, 1969.

Tait, Malcolm. "The Facts of Art Are Life." *Music Educators Journal* 60, no. 5 (January 1974): 33-37.

Tall, Johannes. "Where Music Begins." *Music Educators Journal* 59, no. 6 (February 1973): 61.

Tanglewood Symposium. "Music in American Society." *Music Educators Journal* 54, no. 3 (November 1967).

Taylor, Elizabeth Medert. "Teach Music Concepts through Body Movement." *Music Educators Journal* 59, no. 8 (April 1973): 50-53.

Thatcher, David A. *Teaching, Loving and Self-Directed Learning.* Pacific Palisades, Calif.: Goodyear Publishing Co., 1973.

_____. "Teachers Live with Mystery." *Educational Leadership,* April 1971, pp. 739-742.

Thompson, James J. *Beyond Words.* New York: Scholastic Magazines, Citation Press, 1973.

Toffler, Alvin. "The Psychology of the Future." In *Learning for Tomorrow.* New York: Random House, Vintage Books, 1974.

Torrance, E. Paul, and Myers, R. E. *Creative Learning and Teaching.* New York: Dodd, Mead, & Co., 1970.

_____. *Encouraging Creativity in the Classroom*. Dubuque, Iowa: William C. Brown Co., 1970.

Tournier, Paul. *Fatigue in Modern Society*. Richmond, Va.: John Knox Press, 1969.

Usher, John F., J. "Music Education in an Age of Ferment." *Music Educators Journal* 54, no. 6 (February 1968): 89-91.

Van Sickle, Dr. "Suzuki Principles Not New." *Gopher Music Notes* 26, no. 2 (December 1969): 5.

Vaughan, Margery M. "Cultivating Creative Behavior." *Music Educators Journal* 59, no. 8 (April 1973): 36.

Weil, Andrew. "The Natural Mind." *Psychology Today* 6, no. 5 (October 1972): 51-97.

Weiner, Daniel N., and Phillips, E. Lakin. *Training in Self-Discipline and Self-Control*. Englewood Cliffs, N.J.: Prentice-Hall, 1971.

Weinstein, Gerald, and Fantini, Mario D., eds. *Toward Humanistic Education: A Curriculum of Affect*. New York: Praeger Publishers, 1970.

Welsbacher, Betty. "Music With Meaning: Special Education." *Gopher Music Notes* 28, no. 4 (April 1972): 7-9.

Westlake, Helen Gum. *Relationships: A Study in Human Behavior*. Lexington, Mass.: Ginn and Co., 1972.

Whalen, Anita. "A Misbehaving Child Only Wants Attention." Part 2. *Keyboard Arts* 3, no. 3 (Autumn 1974): 13-14.

Wiley, Dan. "Teaching Music to the Blind." *Clavier* 7, no. 8 (November 1968): 14-17.

Woodruff, Asabel D. "Open Up the Well of Feelings." *Music Educators Journal* 58, no. 1 (September 1971): 22.

Zabrach, Harold. "The Musical Encounter Experience." *Clavier* 12, no. 4 (April 1973): 39-47.

Zavalloni, Roberto. *Self Determination*. Chicago: Forum Books, 1962.

Zimmerman, George H. "A Danger to Musical Art?" *Music Educators Journal* 60, no. 2 (October 1973): 68-69.